THE ART OF WAR FOR
SMALL BUSINESS

THE ART OF WAR

FOR

SMALL BUSINESS

Defeat the Competition and Dominate
the Market with the Masterful Strategies of
SUN TZU

Becky Sheetz-Runkle

AMACOM

AMERICAN MANAGEMENT ASSOCIATION

New York • Atlanta • Brussels • Chicago • Mexico City • San Francisco
Shanghai • Tokyo • Toronto • Washington, D.C.

This publication is designed to provide accurate and authoritative information in regard to the subject matter covered. It is sold with the understanding that the publisher is not engaged in rendering legal, accounting, or other professional service. If legal advice or other expert assistance is required, the services of a competent professional person should be sought.

© 2014 Becky Sheetz-Runkle.
All rights reserved.
Printed in the United States of America.

LIBRARY OF CONGRESS CATALOGING-IN-PUBLICATION DATA
Sheetz-Runkle, Becky.
The art of war for small business : defeat the competition and dominate the market with the masterful strategies of Sun Tzu / Becky Sheetz-Runkle.—1 Edition.
pages cm
Includes bibliographical references and index.
ISBN-13: 978-0-8144-3381-2
ISBN-10: 0-8144-3381-2
1. Small business—Management. 2. Strategic planning. 3. Leadership. I. Title.
HD62.7S5254 2014
658.4'012—dc23   2014005358

About AMA

American Management Association (www.amanet.org) is a world leader in talent development, advancing the skills of individuals to drive business success. Our mission is to support the goals of individuals and organizations through a complete range of products and services, including classroom and virtual seminars, webcasts, webinars, podcasts, conferences, corporate and government solutions, business books, and research. AMA's approach to improving performance combines experiential learning—learning through doing—with opportunities for ongoing professional growth at every step of one's career journey.

Printing number
10 9 8 7 6 5 4 3 2 1

To my husband, David Runkle.
He deserves a medal.

CONTENTS

PART 3—PRINCIPLES FOR THE BATTLEFIELD

PART 4—ADVANCED SUN TZU: STRATEGY FOR YOUR SMALL BUSINESS

ACKNOWLEDGMENTS

The Art of War for Small Business relies on Lionel Giles's translation as its primary source. I am also deeply indebted to Thomas Huynh for his translated and annotated *The Art of War: Spirituality for Conflict,* published by SkyLight Paths Publishing, and for generously allowing me to use many passages from his work here. Thomas has been a source of encouragement and understanding of Sun Tzu, and his perspective brings a more nuanced view of the philosopher-general. I've made some reference to the popular translation by Samuel B. Griffith of Oxford University, as well as the version presented to Steven Michaelson in Beijing at a symposium of the Research Society of Sun Tzu's *Art of War.* I also relied on J. H. Huang's *Sun-Tzu: Art of War—The New Translation,* published by Harper Paperbacks, for some translations as well as difficult-to-find historical context.

I am grateful to each of these authors for their contributions to the Sun Tzu literature and for their guidance in developing *The Art of War for Small Business.*

THE ART OF WAR FOR
SMALL BUSINESS

INTRODUCTION

Imagine that the great strategy mastermind Sun Tzu was with us today. Imagine that he, like a lot of career military men and women, went into business later in life as a CEO or joined the executive team of a small business. How would he adapt his principles from *The Art of War* to wage war and peace for his small business and build it into an empire?

That's the question at the heart of *The Art of War for Small Business*.

The military principles of Sun Tzu's classic, *The Art of War*, are timeless. They're adapted and brought to life daily by the companies and executives that use them. Sound strategists frequently bring Sun Tzu to life, often without necessarily recognizing the origins of their strategy in the sage's words from more than 2,500 years ago. How much more effective would they be if they studied Sun Tzu's direction and were able to apply it more intentionally? How much more effective would you be?

Small-business leaders must be smarter and stealthier than their larger, better-established adversaries. They'll fail if they try to match the big players tool for tool and move for move. And they'll wither on the vine if they just attempt to weather storms. This is particularly true in competitive industries with small and shrinking margins. Small businesses must win battles and achieve success with very lean budgets and comparatively few resources. The great news is that if interpreted and explained well, Sun Tzu provides profound insight to direct and inspire the moves of small-business leaders so that they can defeat their competition and dominate their markets.

To make Sun Tzu as relevant as possible, *The Art of War for Small Business* is filled with examples of his strategies put into play by small businesses. In most (though not all) cases, the practitioners have probably emulated our hero unwittingly, but they've been rewarded for their movements all the same. Some of these businesses have missed the mark later in their evolution, and others may fall from grace, either temporarily or permanently, in the future. But don't mistake future pitfalls with performance that's worth learning from and perhaps emulating.

The Art of War for Small Business is for current and aspiring entrepreneurs and small-business practitioners who are battling Goliaths, and who one day seek to become powerhouses in their respective industries. It's also for those who study Sun Tzu and are looking for a new adaptation uniquely for smaller forces. This book is a comprehensive study of Sun Tzu's masterpiece, targeted to applications for small armies and illustrated with success stories. *The Art of War* is very much the playbook that smaller forces can use for domination. This book is your guide to its application.

SUN TZU IN JUJITSU

I took my very first martial arts lesson in 1990. I was fifteen, and it was a defining moment. Most people take a lesson in karate, tae kwon do, jujitsu, or another martial art and, if they like it, declare that they want to get a black belt. Not me. It was during that very first Tang Soo Do class at the now-defunct Rising Sun Karate Club that I knew I wanted to do martial arts. I wanted to study and to train and teach. I knew the very first night that I would one day have my own school. More than twenty years and several black belts later, I'm pleased to say that dreams come true and that passion can continue to burn. I teach at a small *dojo* (training hall) in my home to a select group of students. But the story hasn't gone as planned.

In those early days, I was fortunate to find an excellent karate school, run by two wonderful instructors, John Weaver and Jack Lynch, both of whom have long since retired from teaching. They started me out on my pursuit of martial arts. I was extremely committed to karate and took that training very, very seriously. I was young and limber, and got pretty good at performing the kicks and punches. I also got quite good at *kata,* a prescribed sequence of movements that gets practiced routinely. But where I fell short, time and time again, was in sparring. I wasn't afraid to fight, and I wasn't afraid to get knocked around. But the bottom line was that when I went toe-to-toe with bigger, stronger opponents, they almost always beat me. They punched harder. They kicked harder. I couldn't outmuscle them. I couldn't outwrestle them. My technical proficiency was no match for their greater strength and size. Despite how hard I worked and trained, the tools I had to use weren't bringing me any closer to reaching my goal of self-defense domination. After Rising Sun Karate Club closed its doors, I trained at a couple of other karate schools in and around rural Lancaster County, Pennsylvania, where I lived.

When I went away to college in Philadelphia, I met Sensei Randy Hutchins. He taught jujitsu—more specifically Sho Bushido Ryu Jujitsu, an aiki-jujitsu that emphasizes concepts such as unbalancing the attacker and using his energy against him. Whereas the karate I studied was linear, jujitsu is circular. Whereas karate is defined by throwing a series of attacks, jujitsu is fluid, with a beginning and an end, but no real steps in the middle. Each technique is one movement.

The karate I studied was based on force against force. The attacker comes in with a powerful blow and you block it, and you deliver your own blow. For me, when the adversary was much stronger, I was on the losing end more often than was acceptable. This was the case no matter how much I trained. I tried for years to make the force-on-force model work for me and fell short. It's very discouraging to pour yourself into something and not see results comparable with the hard work and commitment you contribute. But my jujitsu experience was far different. It isn't based on force vs. force. Instead, you blend with your attacker, break his balance, disorient him, and render him compliant. And if you're good, it looks and feels effortless. I've found this type of martial arts to be much better suited for me to prepare for extremely challenging self-defense scenarios and dealing with stronger, bigger adversaries. But it was difficult. The aspects of karate in which I excelled came easily for me. Leaving those principles to adopt new ones that were diametrically opposed to what I knew was intimidating and uncomfortable. But it has made all the difference.

My martial arts journey has required some serious and unanticipated course changes that called me to question what I knew and understood. How does my experience relate to your small business? In the same way, you may need to make some changes that are painful and abandon some practices to which you've grown very attached. Practices you probably take for granted as truth. They need to be exchanged for a spirit of flexibility, adaptability, and willingness to branch out—in some cases quite radically—so that innovation can flourish. You need a clear sense of your strategic objectives and an insightful picture of your organization and competitors, which requires an honest assessment of your battlefield. Let Sun Tzu illuminate that path.

PART ONE

SEIZE THE ADVANTAGE WITH SUN TZU

Within the context of an overview of Sun Tzu and *The Art of War*, as presented in the first two chapters, you'll explore the critical and common advantages and disadvantages of the small business. They will be recurring factors throughout the book, building blocks toward the more advanced concepts. You'll understand the impact of *The Art of War* on generations and learn how to use *The Art of War for Small Business*. You'll learn about my translation methodology and receive some warnings on how *not* to study Sun Tzu, no matter how tempting.

1

ABOUT SUN TZU AND
THE ART OF WAR

This chapter covers fundamental background on Sun Tzu and *The Art of War*. It provides you an understanding of the high-level historical context that will set the stage for the lessons you can apply to your small business.

ABOUT SUN TZU

Sun Tzu was a contemporary of Confucius. He is believed to have lived from 544 to 496 BC, near the end of the spring and autumn period, during tumultuous times in China. During this period of the weak Chou dynasty, China had more than 150 states continually competing for power. These states battled one another until only thirteen major ones remained. Of these, seven had far superior troops and resources. This era set the stage for the Warring States period that would follow.[1]

Sun Tzu is the name we associate with *The Art of War*. His given name was Sun Wu. He was born into a noble clan with the surname Chen. A student of military theory, he traveled to the state of Wu as its military power was poised to escalate. Impressed with Sun Tzu, the king of Wu brought him into the fold to head up troop discipline and to assist General Wu Zixu in creating the state's strategy for expansion.[2]

Wu's foremost rival was the state of Chu. Because Chu was a superpower, the king of Wu, General Wu, and Sun Tzu knew they'd need to carefully conceive and execute a strategy to defeat their stronger foe. So they split their armies into three and conducted hit-and-run attacks on the mighty Chu. For five years, Wu used this strategy. It worked like this: A division of Wu would approach Chu, and the superpower would emerge. Wu would then withdraw. Then, when Chu would withdraw, Wu would emerge. For five years, Wu did this, seeking to exhaust and agitate its foes, hopeful that they would make mistakes.[3] It worked. Chu experienced great losses. Then, in the sixth year, 506 BC, Wu launched a decisive assault, won all five battles, and took Ying, Chu's capital.[4]

ABOUT *THE ART OF WAR*

As the earliest and most enduring book on strategy,[5] and certainly one of the foremost works for the battlefield, *The Art of War* is the authoritative guide for military affairs and political activities in the Far East, and it has become a prominent and oft-studied treatise in military, political, and business settings all over the world. While *The Art of War* is a short and concise text of about 7,000 words, its contents are immeasurably dense and its applications infinite.

The Art of War is required reading in many business schools and military institutions and essential reading for business leaders. We have no way of knowing just how many forces over the centuries have applied Sun Tzu. The work was first translated into French in 1772, and the first complete and annotated English translation was published by Lionel Giles in 1910. *The Art of War* was used with considerable success by the North Vietnamese during the Vietnam War. It's said that it was that war that first brought Sun Tzu to the attention of the American military. General Vo Nguyen Giap successfully implemented tactics described in *The Art of War* during the Battle of Dien Bien Phu, a turning point that ended the major French involvement. General Vo, later the military mastermind behind victories over American forces in Vietnam, was an avid student and practitioner of Sun Tzu's ideas. *The Art of War* is well cited as influencing Mao Tse-tung and other communist insurgencies. Two American generals, Norman Schwarzkopf and Colin Powell, applied Sun Tzu during the first Gulf War.[6]

But it is Sun Tzu's enduring business context that is of greatest interest to us here.

Sun Tzu is studied in MBA courses throughout the United States and by multinational corporations. Small businesses are especially well served to use this text to understand war as a metaphor for business. Today, many companies of all sizes are basing their growth on principles such as ecosystem development, strategic alliances and networks, transparent user communities, and open innovation. Such concepts may, at first, appear contrary to military strategy. Wouldn't Sun Tzu be better suited to the dictatorial leadership style that was more in vogue in previous generations? That assumption demonstrates a limited understanding of the sage. And certainly this manner of waging business is inadequate for the collaborative, open, dynamic ways in which small businesses are thriving today.

SUN TZU FOR SMALL BUSINESS: STRATEGY AND SERENDIPITY

There are many books that apply Sun Tzu to business, as well as other pursuits. My initial adaptation was *Sun Tzu for Women: The Art of War for Winning in Business.* Are authors being opportunistic? Maybe. But I can only speak for myself. Here's the truth. *Sun Tzu for Women* fell into my lap, so to speak. It wasn't my concept, but an opportunity presented itself that, upon close examination, was very attractive. As I studied *The Art of War,* this time with a renewed focus on its implications for women in business, I saw that application. But that wasn't all that I saw.

As I was writing *Sun Tzu for Women,* I was repeatedly struck by how his principles could shape and build smaller forces into mighty organizations. I thought of all the entrepreneurs and small-business CEOs and leaders I've worked with and for over the years. Before writing that book, I had reread *The Art of War* shortly after cofounding a small agency, Q2 Marketing, which we later sold in 2011. At that time, my perspective was as a new entrepreneur entering a large but crowded space. I studied it within a competitive context. But today, I read it differently. I see it through the lens of a marketing and strategy consultant, and through my clients' eyes. I think you'll find that Sun Tzu's *The Art of War* has profound application for your small business, too.

The Art of War has helped me to identify and seize opportunities, and it's guided me to create favorable conditions for victory. It can help you to take advantage of every opportunity. And as you'll see, equipping a smaller force to overtake a larger one is a central and enduring theme of Sun Tzu.

2

THE POWER OF APPLYING *THE ART OF WAR FOR SMALL BUSINESS*

We take our perspectives everywhere we go. Everything we say and do is autobiographical. If you want to read *The Art of War* as a book on winning and keeping peace, you can. You can read it as a book of aggression. I'm a lifelong martial artist, small-business and marketing practitioner, and history enthusiast. I respect "just wars" and the soldiers who fight them and, like Sun Tzu, I believe that war is best when it's uncommon. As I closely follow public policy in the international arena, I understand the threat and reality of war as a historical constant. The weak are overrun by the strong. People everywhere are in a state of competition.

Business, too, in many ways, is like war. Small businesses that endeavor to fight by the rules set up by industry powerhouses are destined for defeat or, at the very least, ghastly carnage. But *The Art of War,* if studied carefully and applied well, can be the winner's manual for ambitious, innovative, and savvy small businesses.

Because Sun Tzu clearly understood how strategy can trump a much larger, better-funded, more powerful adversary, his counsel is eminently well suited for small-business leaders who do battle with larger opponents. It's also suited for small businesses in competitive markets that consist of other small and mid-tier players that seek to dominate. Thomas Huynh, author of *The Art of War: Spirituality for Conflict* and founder of Sonshi, an educational resource, understands that Sun Tzu's intended audience in writing his work was weaker forces. The sage sought to teach those in disadvantaged positions how to seize the advantageous position.[1] The author of his book's foreword, Marc Benioff, CEO of Salesforce.com, whom you'll read more about later in these pages, agrees: "Fundamentally," Benioff writes, "the book demonstrates how small armies can defeat larger ones."[2]

Sun Tzu is an architect of grand strategy. Yet existing business books on Sun Tzu don't tell us how big players used grand strategy to become industry powerhouses. They tell how the big businesses became even bigger, or mistakes they made that caused them to fall. That's why the objective here is to exercise a lesson from Sun Tzu and fill the void by showing small-business practitioners how to learn from counterparts that have grown their territories based on modern illustrations of Sun Tzu. You have before you a new concept for the business world, and its time has come.

SUN TZU FOR MODERN BUSINESS WARFARE

Large advertising and promotional budgets no longer dictate a company's credibility. Savvy small businesses use cost-effective guerilla marketing techniques to compete with the massive budgets of their competitors. Low-budget 5-Hour Energy commercials were chastised by the ad industry. Chobani used an extra-large cup mold and a shiny label that stood out in the dairy case from all the other yogurts.[3] When Boston Beer Company began to expand outside of New England, the company's founder flew to Washington, DC, to sell the flagship Samuel Adams to bars. He flew so frequently that Presidential Airlines began selling Samuel Adams on its planes, and he even got the beer's name printed on the back of the ticket jackets.[4]

It takes this kind of innovation and stretching of resources to stand out. Today, you can increasingly go directly to the customer, at a lower cost than ever before. When customers compare products, they look at online and social media presence. They compare positive and negative rankings on the web, including your number of social media followers and how fans interact on your Facebook page. Humble Seed is a start-up that provides high-quality organic seed varieties. It acquired ten new wholesale accounts because of the volume of its Facebook fan base, which is currently just short of 35,000. The company now competes with larger brands.[5]

Small businesses won't gain market share by battling larger adversaries head-on. Consider the example of Felix Dennis, CEO of Dennis Publishing. His firm battled powerhouse Ziff Davis in the consumer technology publishing industry and fought bitterly. Dennis won, but the costs were tremendous—two years of profits for his entire company.[6] Sun Tzu would have deemed this approach a colossal waste of money and resources, and, in retrospect, Dennis agrees. The small businesses that win do so by building strategic alliances, outmaneuvering the larger businesses, creating opportunities, outperforming, and by taking advantage of every opportunity within their grasp. Sun Tzu has never been more relevant for small businesses seeking to seize every advantage.

PRIMARY SMALL-BUSINESS ADVANTAGES

The extent to which a business understands and leverages its competitive advantages will determine its success. While small businesses playing in competitive markets often find themselves at a stark disadvantage, collectively, they have general strengths that they must recognize and to which they must play. The most common advantages of small companies vis-à-vis larger entities, regardless of the industry they serve, are listed here. These advantages will be detailed and applied against the backdrop of Sun Tzu throughout the chapters that follow.

- Alliance building
- Agility and speed of movement
- Consensus-building ease
- Excitement and enthusiasm of new and young companies and ideas
- Flexibility in processes and procedures
- Iconoclastic worldview and readiness to take on all comers
- Independence
- Intimate knowledge of customers
- Innovation and nurturing of ideas
- Niche exploitation
- Openness to taking risks
- Power of the unexpected
- Unity of purpose and commitment to mission

PRIMARY SMALL-BUSINESS DISADVANTAGES

Throughout my career as a strategic marketing and communications consultant and in working for ad agencies, I've supported hundreds of small-business leaders. Time and again, they fall into the same patterns of the crippling mistakes Sun Tzu warns against. To anyone familiar with the paradoxes of small business, it's no surprise that some of the disadvantages listed here are also on the advantage list.

- Competitive job field with employees who can be wooed away by bigger companies
- Competitive partner and vendor field, with partners that may give their best to the industry leader
- Desire to close sales, even on products or services that aren't profitable or part of a long-term plan
- Failure to consolidate gains due to lack of long-range focus
- Fear of standing out, putting a stake in the ground, and being "too different"
- Lack of organizational unified purpose
- Lack of structure and hierarchy
- Less cash flow
- Less developed processes and systems
- Less experienced leadership and management
- Limited resources
- Limited/underdeveloped understanding of the competitive field
- Decision making that's based on false yet deeply held assumptions
- Perceived and real risk of doing business with a smaller firm
- Poor emphasis on strategy
- Priorities that shift continually with the pursuit of opportunities
- Small footprint within the industry and less clout

BIG BUSINESS DISADVANTAGES

If we look at the small-business disadvantages and turn them around, we get a good picture of the advantages many of the larger players possess. But let's do something a little less demoralizing and look at where big players most commonly fall short. These liabilities will surface and be explored throughout *The Art of War for Small Business*.

Narrow focus on core products and customers. Publicly traded big businesses are under tremendous pressure to show revenue and earnings growth each and every quarter. The most effective way to achieve this growth consistently, quarter by quarter, is to focus most aggressively on their biggest opportunities in their most reliable core markets. This has the natural consequence of leading big businesses to tend to their biggest products, platforms, channels, and customers. For smaller competitors, this situation presents potential to deliver on smaller opportunities with customers that are less attractive to the big businesses.

Difficulty adapting. The advantage for the big guys is in economies of scale and scope that enable them to offer lower costs while reaping the rewards of better margins. The cost of these rewards has often been that the machine behind these products and services is a labyrinth that includes (or ensnares) various areas of the company, such as manufacturing, marketing, sales, distribution, and finance. This complexity and interdependency makes it difficult, expensive, and risky to change.

Aversion to risk. It's far more difficult for large organizations to tolerate risk than it is for smaller ones. They simply have much more to lose. Big businesses are more inclined to accept lower-risk concepts than new ideas that involve greater risk. Sir James Dyson, who achieved massive success on the heels of more than 5,000 "failures" in pursuit of the bagless vacuum cleaner, has said, "Big companies tend not to take risks, so there's a big opportunity for entrepreneurs to take them and march on competitors."[7] Smaller organizations looking to edge out much larger counterparts must have a greater propensity for failure.

Some larger businesses maintain their emphasis on innovation and are equipped to tolerate risk, however. Beginning in its early days, Salesforce.com leveraged its comparatively smaller size to create an advantage that allowed the business to quickly and smartly innovate while flying under the radar of its market's Goliaths. Salesforce succeeded by doing something entirely new in a market that already existed, and by doing it in a way that was very difficult for anyone else to copy.[8] And as innovation expert Clayton Christensen has noted, Salesforce continues to nurture this spirit of innovation, even as the company has grown into a billion-dollar player.[9]

SMALL BUSINESSES NEED SUN TZU

Too many small businesses appear to operate as if they have little or no strategic focus. When you get close to many of these organizations, you understand that the appearance is often the reality. They sacrifice strategy for making short-term tactical moves. But winning strategy can't come out of applying the same methods and hopes week after week, month after month. Tactics are critical, but if these steps aren't being carried out in support of sound strategy, it's a lot of activity without a lot of progress.

Does that ring true for your business sometimes? More than sometimes?

Your company must have a real-world strategic plan that carefully considers the reality of your competitive marketplace. With that plan in place, each department within the organization should have a well-coordinated strategic plan and tactics to support the company's über-goal. Everything you do should be designed to deploy and advance that strategy. I think we all know this at our core, but we don't all run our businesses like we know it to be true. If we did, business coaching wouldn't be a multibillion-a-year industry.[10]

THE WAR METAPHOR TODAY

There are obviously some things that Sun Tzu would do differently on a business battlefield today than on a literal battleground 2,500 years ago in warring China. He'd continue to emphasize the role of supreme strategy in defeating the "enemy," or perhaps he'd update the language to say "competition." Maybe. He'd maintain his emphasis on gaining intelligence, taking advantage of alliances, outmaneuvering the competition, taking the better position, dividing and overtaking a larger enemy, and he'd remind us of the necessary characteristics of an effective leader. But he'd also talk a great deal about an entirely new constituency of no consequence to the military reader of antiquity: the customer. This group will be very important to us as we apply these principles.

HOW TO READ *THE ART OF WAR FOR SMALL BUSINESS*

This book is composed of four parts: 1) Seize the Advantage with Sun Tzu; 2) Understanding: Essential Sun Tzu; 3) Principles for the Battlefield; and 4) Advanced Sun Tzu: Strategy for Your Small Business. Within these sections, we explore twelve key themes from *The Art of War* that are expressly for small-business leaders and entrepreneurs. The objective is to help you build a stronger, more enduring, more successful business.

There are many good and inexpensive English-language translations of *The Art of War*. I have relied largely on the popular Lionel Giles translation, which was the first complete English-language work of the classic. I've also carefully studied and compared many credible and even somewhat divergent translations, including those of Huynh, Griffith, Huang, and the version Michaelson received in Beijing at a symposium of the Research Society of Sun Tzu's *Art of War*. Unless otherwise noted, the excerpts used here are from Giles's translation. This work is available in the public domain for free.

A great deal is written and said about Sun Tzu. Much of it is in quotes and passages haphazardly passed around the Internet like fourth-generation hand-me-downs in a very big family. These pearls of "wisdom" are attributed to him and *The Art of War*. But many of these attributions are poor interpretations and others are statements that do not, in any way, appear in *The Art of War*. Be careful with the Sun Tzu you apply to your business. Stick to reputable translations and you'll be on the right track.

Naturally, throughout this book I've opted to use masculine pronouns in reference to Sun Tzu's general and his army. That shouldn't be surprising, as the text was written in the same way. Don't allow that to narrow the intended application of *The Art of War for Small Business*.

One more note: Some of the concepts I'll share will be repetitive. That sometimes irritates me as a reader of business books. I want the author to make her point and move on, and stop filling pages with the same ideas. Sun Tzu drew some repeated conclusions in his very short work. So when you see the same theme restated again or in another chapter, there's a very good reason for it. And it's not to fill pages.

SUN TZU'S FIVE CONSTANT FACTORS

The Art of War opens with Sun Tzu's statement of the five constant factors. It's on these factors, and other unifying principles, that I base the twelve themes of this book.

> The art of war, then, is governed by five constant factors, to be taken into account in one's deliberations, when seeking to determine the conditions obtained in the field. These are: (1) The Moral Law; (2) Heaven; (3) Earth; (4) The Commander; (5) method and discipline.

Let's explore these five factors:

1. The Moral Law causes the people to be in complete accord with their ruler, so that they will follow him regardless of their lives, undismayed by any danger. Thomas Huynh interprets moral law as "The Way." Moral law governs the leader's character, shapes method and discipline, and impacts success. Sun Tzu says later about the moral law:

> *The consummate leader cultivates the moral law, and strictly adheres to method and discipline; thus it is in his power to control success.*

There is doubtlessly a moral, and I believe, an intended spiritual element here that will be adhered to and applied in accordance with each reader's belief system. We can also take the moral law to apply to the unity of purpose a small business needs to serve its customers and employees with distinction.

2. Heaven signifies night and day, cold and heat, times and seasons. According to Griffith, the Chinese character T'ien (Heaven) is used in this verse to mean "weather." The application here for you is in timing of maneuvers, amid considerations of market factors and conditions that influence them.[11]

3. Earth comprises distances, great and small; danger and security; open ground and narrow passes; the chances of life and death. This statement reflects the importance of maneuvering effectively and knowing the advantages and disadvantages of different types of terrain.

4. The Commander stands for the virtues of wisdom, sincerely, benevolence, courage, and strictness. A full picture of Sun Tzu's general is covered in Chapter 7, "Embody the General."

5. Method and discipline are to be understood [as] the marshaling of the army in its proper subdivisions, the graduations of rank among the officers, the maintenance of roads by which supplies may reach the army, and the control of military expenditure. Discipline, structure, and organization are paramount for Sun Tzu.

Of these five factors, Sun Tzu says:

> . . . [H]e who knows them will be victorious; he who knows them not will fail.

Let's now delve more deeply into Sun Tzu's *Art of War* and how it can help you dominate your market. We'll begin by looking at the philosopher-general's essential counsel for understanding, beginning with your organization and extending out to all the audiences that matter to your success.

PART TWO

UNDERSTANDING: ESSENTIAL SUN TZU

The next four chapters contain some of the most oft-cited passages that are the essential building blocks of *The Art of War*. The chapters in Part 2 will guide you through what Sun Tzu directs on the importance of developing a complete, honest, and uncompromising understanding of yourself and your business, your enemy, your market, and your assets: customers, employees, and partners. This material is fundamental, but don't mistake that with easy. These ideas must be carefully studied. If you avoid these directives, you do so at your business's peril.

Just about every business leader would probably agree that an understanding of these factors makes eminently good sense. But application is in an entirely different league. Leaders of small businesses tend to make assumptions about what they believe is true about the market, their businesses, their products, their competitors, and their people. They are sure they know why their customers buy from them, and how their products best meet customer needs. If they can't see past their often false assumptions, they won't be prepared for the battles that are ahead. They'll be vulnerable to competitors who take seriously the charge to truly understand their organizations, marketplace, and customers.

Consider carefully this imperative passage as we prepare to explore this section:

> *If you know the enemy and know yourself, you need not fear the result of a hundred battles. If you know yourself but not the enemy, for every victory gained you will also suffer a defeat. If you know neither the enemy nor yourself, you will succumb in every battle.*

3

UNDERSTAND YOURSELF

F ull, complete, and actionable knowledge of the army is fundamental for Sun Tzu. Similarly, you can never effectively act on any understanding of your enemy or your market without a thorough understanding of your organization. If you can't honestly assess where you're strong and where you're weak, any victory you achieve will be fleeting.

BRUTAL HONESTY: OVERCOME FALSE ASSUMPTIONS

False assumptions are the self-perpetuating common plague of some small-business leaders. If the assumers aren't careful, they'll hear and parrot the same party lines again and again and pass these misguided ideas onto the entire team. This path serves to further isolate leadership from actual marketplace facts by allowing people to continue to draw mistaken conclusions. I've seen many small businesses completely misunderstand their marketplace because they didn't want to believe that their products or services were missing the mark, or they didn't want to make the necessary investments for course corrections, or they simply didn't offer the innovation or differentiation that they thought they did.

Always hold your beliefs about your business and its performance up against real-world data, and when the two are in conflict, pay attention.

SUN TZU'S FIVE ESSENTIALS FOR VICTORY

Sun Tzu said that there are five concepts for winning. Each has at its core the general's understanding of his army.

1. *He will win who knows when to fight and when not to fight.*

    This concept will be covered in Chapter 8, "Perseverance."

2. *He will win who knows how to handle both superior and inferior forces.*

    This concept is also popularly translated as "large and small forces."

3. *He will win whose army is animated by the same spirit throughout all its ranks.*

    This idea of unity through the ranks will be expounded on in Chapter 10.

4. *He will win who, prepared himself, waits to take the enemy unprepared.*

Sun Tzu advises to pick the right timing and catch your adversaries when they aren't ready. But that strategy can't be optimized if leadership isn't prepared to maximize that opportunity.

5. *He will win who has military capacity and is not interfered with by the sovereign.*

This last essential is manifold. Strong leaders hold fast to their principles and want what is good for the organization. Sun Tzu's general must have a capable army, and be unencumbered by bureaucracy, so he can make decisions. Leaders must be driven by principles and act in the best interests of the organization. However, they can't make the best day-to-day or long-term decisions for that organization unless their knowledge of it is deep.

Sun Tzu follows these essentials with this "so what":

Hence the saying: If you know the enemy and know yourself, you need not fear the result of a hundred battles. If you know yourself but not the enemy, for every victory gained you will also suffer a defeat. If you know neither the enemy nor yourself, you will succumb in every battle.

A FLOOR WAX AND A DESSERT TOPPING!

It's critical to understand what your organization is and does, as well as what it isn't and doesn't do. The all-things-to-all-people trap can be a barrier to understanding and clearly defining an organization's offerings. Fearful of losing a sale, small-business leaders can be unwilling to put a stake in the ground and say,

"We sell product or service X to this market." That bold declaration doesn't just define what you sell and to whom; just as important, it defines what you do not sell and to whom you do not sell. This statement requires an appreciation for solutions and markets that are profitable, and those that are not.

I worked with a consulting company that focused on the federal sector. The owners and leadership had built a healthy midsize business, but they realized they had a problem. They grew their business based on one customer. That customer's myriad needs took them away from their primary focus and into tangential lines of business. If you're trying to grow your business, you may see this as a pretty good problem to have. And it was, to a point. The rub was the realization that they had moved into places that they didn't really want to be, and that it wasn't serving to strategically grow the company. Contracts were increasingly comprised of lower-skilled, low-margin solutions that were not easily repeatable for other customers. Meanwhile, they had a highly skilled workforce that was growing increasingly frustrated, so this trend was doubly damaging. To combat this tendency of looking at the short-term contract value and simply saying "yes" to the customer without thinking of the long-term impact to the organization, the leaders of this business undertook a significant restructuring to expand into other areas.

In another common example, a small business I worked with cast a wide net in an effort to miss no opportunities. That sounds good, but not everything that parades as an opportunity really is. And sometimes, you should be able to tell pretty easily that some floats shouldn't be allowed anywhere near the parade. This company targeted mid- and large-tier hospitals and healthcare practices. The company had an excellent concept, but the CEO's focus shifted with the weather. Rather than politely telling small practices, including very small ones, that they weren't a fit for the company's solutions or price point, he chose to capture their information and add them to the pipeline with a pipe dream that "a solution for your market is on the way." In reality, the organization wasn't able to consistently deliver to the larger-tier clients it signed up, and for which it had dedicated tens of thousands of development hours. It didn't have the infrastructure to support sales and service to a very different client base, particularly one that wouldn't be profitable.

Mega retail stores may be able to have something for nearly everyone, but small businesses can't, and trying to do so will only confuse the organization's mission and message, and add layers of complexity. And complexity kills sales. Ideas are cheap. Resist the temptation to start with a floor wax product but then conceive of an opportunity to make the same product into a dessert topping, or offer it all under the same confused banner. It's tempting to fall into the trap of trying to be all things to all people, in an attempt not to lose any opportunities. But small businesses have to remember that not everything is an "opportunity" if it doesn't fit into your organization's goals and objectives.

COMPENSATING FOR WEAKNESS WITH STRENGTH

This somewhat obscure Sun Tzu idea speaks to adaptability to threats.

> The skillful tactician may be likened to the shuai-jan. Now the shuai-jan is a snake that is found in the Chung mountains. Strike at its head, and you will be attacked by its tail; strike at its tail, and you will be attacked by its head; strike at its middle, and you will be attacked by head and tail both.

A precursor to being able to adapt is awareness of your organizational weaknesses and strengths. Cross-functional training and unity will help your business overcome threats and advance forward.

Atari cofounder Nolan Bushnell understood the bottom-line need to have a well-rounded, cross-trained team. He wasn't satisfied that his team, composed largely of B2B engineers, had no substantive knowledge of their customers' needs. The solution wasn't in a seminar or classroom training. Bushnell sent the engineers into the trenches.

He wanted them to share the experiences of both customers and distributors. To that end, Atari engineers were given responsibility for running games in test locations, with profit-and-loss responsibilities, just like distributors. They learned how to identify problems and defects before they affected customers or distributors. This experience also gave them valuable early insight into which games would be the most successful. Atari even sent its engineers onto rotation on the assembly line, so they could better design products that would be most easily manufactured.

By developing a better understanding of critical pieces of the puzzle—in this case customers, manufacturers, and distributors—Bushnell strengthened the organization and compensated for weak spots.[1]

Only by honestly evaluating and understanding your weaknesses will you be positioned to overcome them.

GET THE BASICS RIGHT

There are some common problem areas, based on false assumptions, that small business leaders must learn to recognize. Missteps in these areas will ultimately cause serious problems.

Gut and Validation

I'm a big believer in trusting your gut and putting your intuition into action for the good of your career or business. A strong gut feeling is very important for many entrepreneurs and innovators. But it may not be enough. Validation from the industry, not only of your concept, but also of how you plan to deliver it, can help affirm your gut instinct and ensure that your concept is deployed well. It's common for entrepreneurs to cling to a flawed concept because it's their baby, even after data and personal experience show them it's not viable. That's not the end of the road (as we'll see in Chapter 12, "Adaptation)", but it will be a death knell if leadership doesn't pivot.

Vague Business Plan

Successful, dynamic businesses have unifying, purposeful objectives. Less successful businesses have vague descriptions of their solutions and lack any differentiation. If your business is looking to get funding, you have to show your depth of knowledge of your business plan, including reliable market projections and an understanding of the competitive landscape. If you can't articulate your plan, you'll have big problems.

Poor Marketplace Understanding

Beware of small-business leaders who boast that they have no competitors. You can't sell and market against other players unless you fully understand what they're selling, how they're delivering it, and who they're selling it to.

A Broken Model

Small businesses need to understand their revenue and profit models so that they'll know if their model is sustainable or will fizzle out well before it takes off. Similarly, your pricing has to be in line with what the market will bear so that it will provide you with a profit. How well does your model work? Really?

KNOW AND LEVERAGE YOUR EMPLOYEES

Fundamental to knowing your organization is understanding and leveraging the mighty force for market domination that is your employee base. Sun Tzu's vision for how soldiers should be treated and led is highly relevant for managing employees and teams. Identifying, hiring, and nurturing talent is even more important for small businesses, where all team members make an exponentially greater contribution to the whole of the organization than their big-business counterparts. Hiring and keeping a poor sales performer, for example, hurts large businesses. But hiring and keeping underperforming sales pros cripples small companies. Yet, it happens all the time. Sun Tzu provides excellent direction on the importance of proper care of the army, as well as positioning all personnel so that they can be eminently effective. Small businesses should apply these concepts to their teams.

Organization and Chain of Command

Order and a chain of command are essential Sun Tzu concepts.

> By method and discipline are to be understood the marshaling of the army in its proper subdivisions, the graduations of rank among

the officers, the maintenance of roads by which supplies may reach the army, and the control of military expenditure.

Without a clear understanding of the approval process and structure by which things get done, organizations will inefficiently spin their wheels, duplicate efforts, and create ineffective lines of communication. This is particularly painful to watch in a small organization, where communication should be smoother and the safeguarding of resources is of the essence.

Sun Tzu further describes one of the ways a ruler can bring misfortune upon his army:

> By employing the officers of his army without discrimination, through ignorance of the military principle of adaptation to circumstances. This shakes the confidence of the soldiers.

Human resources must be dedicated appropriately and most effectively, yet they can be adapted to specific needs as required. If people aren't utilized optimally, their confidence in leadership is weakened and their frustration increases. It's essential that you understand how to best bring out your people's attributes and fully understand their strengths.

Hire Doers over Deliberators

Small businesses need people who can act definitively and get things done.

> If the campaign is protracted, the resources of the State will not be equal to the strain.

It's essential to carefully craft and execute strategy. Although patience and timing are important, when it comes time for action, small businesses need people who are proven and capable performers, and who will take action instead of calling for unnecessary delays or making excuses for not delivering.

Mobilize Strong Teams

Sun Tzu's emphasis is not only on having the right troops, but on leveraging them for maximum impact, especially when it matters most.

> The clever combatant looks to the effect of combined energy, and does not require too much from individuals. Hence his ability to pick out the right men and utilize combined energy. When he utilizes combined energy, his fighting men become as it were like unto rolling logs or stones. For it is the nature of a log or stone to remain motionless on level ground, and to move when on a slope; if four-cornered, to come to a standstill, but if round-shaped, to go rolling down. Thus the energy developed by good fighting men is as the momentum of a round stone rolled down a mountain thousands of feet in height.

The power of the right people, all moving in the right direction, following the right leaders, can't be overstated. This is one of my favorite passages from *The Art of War* because it highlights the exponential power of excellent people when they're led well.

Teams can't be strong unless they're loyal. Zappos, the online shoe and clothing shop with the extraordinary brand that's included in just about any discussion of exceptional customer service, is a well-known success story. In 2009, Zappos was acquired by Amazon.com in an all-stock deal worth about $1.2 billion. The Zappos community, which includes its employees, is the central force behind that hefty price tag. Zappos is famous for its policy of paying its new employees . . . to quit. Once new hires are about a week into training, the company offers them a $2,000 bonus, in addition to compensation for their time worked. All they have to do is quit. This is how Zappos has built a committed, loyal, and high-performing team that spreads that same spirit to the Zappos customer base.[2] Between 2 percent to 3 percent of all would-be new employees accept the offer, according to the Zappos corporate website.[3] Think about it: $2,000 is a small price to pay to rid your business of an employee who won't perform.

In the same way, Jim Koch, the creator of Samuel Adams, always seeks to raise the average with the people Boston Beer Company hires. They've done it by profiling successful employees and developing interview questions that will determine if a candidate has the same motivation and behavioral qualities that will help raise the average.[4]

Consideration of Your People

This passage highlights the leader's responsibility to demonstrate care and concern for your people.

> If you are careful of your men, and camp on hard ground, the army will be free from disease of every kind, and this will spell victory.

This care extends beyond lip service. It must translate into the actions of the leader. Note that the objective remains on winning, and the wise steward of his people recognizes that being careful of his men is a necessary means to that end. This lesson is especially important for small businesses because turnover is expensive and disrupts their ability to innovate and satisfy customer demands. And the cost of your best people going to your competitors is even higher.

Building Incentives

Sun Tzu clearly values his troops and is careful to motivate and incentivize them. Of rewarding the troops he says:

> In chariot fighting, when ten or more chariots have been taken, those should be rewarded who took the first. This is called, using the conquered foe to augment one's own strength.

For twenty-first-century small-business leaders, this idea is less about chariot fighting and more about rewarding your people for acting swiftly, successfully, and exceptionally. This modus operandi applies to all types of businesses. Five Guys awards cash bonuses to crews that score the highest in weekly restaurant audits. These impromptu audits rate bathroom cleanliness, courtesy, food preparation, and kitchen equipment safety. A good score earns $1,000, which gets split among five or six people on a crew. In a recent year, Five Guys awarded more than $11 million to employees for performance.[5]

> When you plunder a countryside, let the spoil be divided amongst your men; when you capture new territory, cut it up into allotments for the benefit of the soldiery.

Sun Tzu directs you to share the fruits of your business's labor, including the opportunity provided by capturing new territory. For a growing business that needs to keep reinvesting in the company, incentives like stock options and performance-based bonuses allow you to reward your women and men, as Sun Tzu advises, without putting an undue burden on the company.

Don't Overdo It

The small businesses that succeed do it because their workforces are driven and work both very hard and very smart. But Sun Tzu warns against overburdening your people and pushing them to:

> . . . make forced marches without halting day or night, covering double the usual distance at a stretch.

Asking too much of them will cause your divisions to fall into the hands of the enemy, prohibit the bulk of your army from reaching its destination, and cause leaders to fall.

> Carefully study the well-being of your men, and do not overtax them. Concentrate your energy and hoard your strength. Keep your army continually on the move, and devise unfathomable plans.

Small organizations know the importance of staying on the move. The most innovative ones are sources of constant motion and creativity. For this reason, you should husband your strength and resources so that you can concentrate energy when it's needed. This requires you to carefully be in tune with the capabilities and limitations of all of your people. The better your leaders know their people and their limitations, the better they'll be able to gauge when undue burden is placed on them, so they can always bring out their best.

Don't Under-Do It

In Chapter 7, we will explore the five dangerous faults that may affect a general. The fifth is *over-solicitude for his men, which exposes him to worry and trouble.*

Small-business leaders can exhibit traits of being excessively concerned with their people's happiness. This tendency can lead them to make decisions based largely on what their people think and feel, at the expense of what's in the best interest of the organization. For Sun Tzu, and for you, neither extreme—pushing your people on forced marches or being excessively concerned for their well-being—is constructive.

Enforcement of Discipline

Not surprisingly, many of Sun Tzu's seven considerations for forecasting victory are centered on the military forces:

1. *Which of the two sovereigns is imbued with the Moral law?*
2. *Which of the two generals has most ability?*
3. *With whom lie the advantages derived from Heaven and Earth?*
4. *On which side is discipline most rigorously enforced?*
5. *Which army is stronger?*
6. *On which side are officers and men more highly trained?*
7. *In which army is there the greater constancy both in reward and punishment?*

Able generals and highly skilled and strong armies are critical. So is the rigorous enforcement of discipline, or consequences.

The idea of order and reward and punishment is as important to Sun Tzu as the character of the sovereign, the general's ability, and the army's strength. Discipline, consistency, and clear communication on expectations are fundamental, but they can be taken for granted by small-business leaders. A shocking number of small businesses propagate a culture of missed deadlines, waffling leadership, insubordination, and negativity. A strong leader will require consistency and make expectations clear.

Sun Tzu provides counsel on how a new leader can incorporate discipline within an organization:

> If soldiers are punished before they have grown attached to you, they will not prove submissive; and, unless submissive, then will be practically useless. If, when the soldiers have become attached to you, punishments are not enforced, they will still be useless.

The direction here is to dole out reprimands appropriately, and only to your people once they have forged a connection with you, not right away just to make a statement. By contrast, if you are unwilling to enforce consequences once your people have identified with your leadership, they won't be assets to you.

Consistency Is Critical

It's essential to deliver clear, consistent communication that's enforced across the organization.

> If a general shows confidence in his men but always insists on his orders being obeyed, the gain will be mutual.

FIVE GUYS

I live in Northern Virginia outside of Washington, DC. I remember when we had one or two Five Guys restaurants here locally. Now they're everywhere. The story of Five Guys is one of doing what you do well, staying in your power lanes, and delivering consistent customer experience. (That's why you'll even learn more about Five Guys, and how they would make Sun Tzu proud, in Chapter 9 "Focus.")

Five Guys is the fastest-growing restaurant chain in the United States, doubling the number of stores since 2009. With revenue in excess of $1 billion in 2012, Five Guys plays in the "better burger" category with burgers in the $8 range. This $2 billion plus segment, of which Five Guys owns nearly half, continues to grow. Not surprisingly, the larger $40 billion category for fast-food burgers in the United States is dominated by McDonald's, Burger King, and Wendy's.[6]

Five Guys has differentiated itself in important and interesting ways. Founder Jerry Murrell didn't invent the "better burger" chain, but his restaurants have been lighting the fire underneath this market category since the middle of the last decade. The category includes In-N-Out Burger, Fuddruckers (my husband's first burger love), and newcomers Smashburger and Shake Shack. Danny Meyer, the New York City restaurateur behind Shake Shack, says he doesn't see Five Guys as a competitor because "a rising tide lifts all burgers." Proving that there's room in the sandbox for others to play, Meyer even spoke at a Five Guys franchisee convention in 2009.[7]

If Meyer has the Five Guys warm and fuzzies, the fast-food giants don't. Five Guys can't compete with the less-better-burgers on price. Instead, McDonald's and Burger King have moved to their versions of "better burgers," introducing higher-quality Angus beef options.[8]

Speaking of quality, "quality control" is what Murrell calls the "magic" of Five Guys. The restaurants don't use any frozen products—at all. Each burger is made to order, and customers can choose from seventeen different toppings. They don't have a drive-through, because the wait would be too long. Restaurants used to post a sign that said, "If you're in a hurry, there are a lot of really good hamburger places within a short distance from here." The message between the lines: This burger is worth getting out of your car and waiting for. And clearly, customers agree.[9]

Five Guys restaurants pay close attention to detail with their burgers, and the same is true of their potato selection and their refusal to have "one frozen thing" in any restaurant, including milk shakes. They will not deliver, either. Murrell told *Inc.* magazine of a call that he personally received from an admiral at the Pentagon. Everyone delivers to the Pentagon, the admiral said. Murrell didn't budge, but he did hang a banner in front of that store that said "ABSOLUTELY NO DELIVERY." Business from the Pentagon has been strong, Murrell said.[10]

While most fast-food chains have transactional relationships with people, Murrell knows that the value of his business is in customers, employees, and suppliers. Five Guys has never had legal problems with franchises. He credits this track record, in part, to quarterly independent franchise committee meetings. They've used many of the same vendors since 1986 because of their commitment to quality and consistent customer experience, not because low cost is the top priority. They also offer incentives to employees for exceptional service.[11]

Five Guys has played its competitive hand with fast-food giants by hiring away some competitors. A past executive from Checkers heads up building new stores, and a former Burger King franchiser now runs the 200 company-owned stores. But knowing the enemy is of little value if you don't understand and leverage your own strengths and assets.

In order to do a few things very, very well, Murrell has succeeded in figuring out what the other players aren't doing, or aren't doing as well, and filling an extremely lucrative void.

SAMUEL ADAMS

Like the patriot his flagship beer is named for, Jim Koch, creator of the Boston Beer Company, has done something quite revolutionary. He's created a high-quality product in an extremely competitive space, and made it ubiquitous to the consumer. But getting his beer into consumers' glasses wasn't easy.

In 1985, when Koch began distributing his sudsy creation, Americans thought the only quality beers were imported. While some consumers would pay more for a Heineken or a Beck's, they were unlikely to pony up a premium price for an American beer. But that resistance was the making of an exciting new niche market. Samuel Adams is seen as an affordable luxury as the beer market, and consumers' palates, continue to evolve.[12]

In the days before the revolution, Boston Beer Company wasn't able to get any local Boston distributors to deliver its brew. So Koch rented a truck and delivered it from bar to bar. At each bar, he'd evangelize about the brewing and ingredient quality, and encourage potential buyers to taste it. This bar-to-bar method worked, as the Sam Adams brand continued to spread the hops of revolution throughout New England and into Washington, DC.[13]

Like Jerry Murrell of Five Guys, Koch has always understood what he was offering to the market. It was flavorful, fresh American beer. Six weeks after Samuel Adams Boston Lager came out, the company won the title of "best beer in America" at the Great American Beer Festival. Koch also understood where his beers fit in the grand scheme. His competition was the imports, not the big American beers. His advice on knowing what you're bringing to market: "If it's not better or cheaper than what's already out there, you don't have a real business to build on."[14]

Today, the movement that Koch created has pulled 2,400 micro-breweries—and counting—along with it in the United States, and that category now owns an impressive 6 percent of the U.S. beer market. Samuel Adams owns one percent of the U.S. beer market. That may sound tiny, but it equated to $629 million in revenue in 2012. It's a stark contrast with the whopping market share of InBev and MillerCoors, but American beer enthusiasts, as well as those in the 20-plus other countries were Samuel Adams beers can be found, owe a debt of gratitude to an originator of the craft beer movement.[15]

4

UNDERSTAND THE ENEMY

How well any business understands its adversaries is a determining factor in whether it wins or loses. Understanding the strengths, weaknesses, and realities of your organization is fundamental, but it is, at best, 50 percent of the equation, as Sun Tzu tells us in this familiar passage:

> If you know the enemy and know yourself, you need not fear the result of a hundred battles.

Sun Tzu's direction on understanding the enemy is foundational to every chapter of *The Art of War*. Here we look at his most essential wisdom on how to develop and apply this knowledge.

CREATE CONDITIONS FOR VICTORY

> If we know that our own men are in a condition to attack, but are unaware that the enemy is not open to attack, we have gone only halfway towards victory.

Your readiness for business battle is only half of the story. While you may be able to keep from being defeated by adopting a defensive strategy that focuses on an insular understanding of your organization, you won't be able to break through to success unless you thoroughly understand your adversary's vulnerabilities and assets. Launching an engagement on an adversary who is strongly positioned could be disastrous for you.

> To secure ourselves against defeat lies in our own hands, but the opportunity of defeating the enemy is provided by the enemy himself.

Being aware of the condition of the competitor's vulnerability is the idea here. You must fully understand the adversary so that you will be able to see those openings. Sun Tzu continues:

> Thus the good fighter is able to secure himself against defeat, but cannot make certain of defeating the enemy. Hence the saying: One may know how to conquer without being able to do it.

How can you guard yourself against defeat and take advantage of the opportunities the enemy offers? Let's explore what Sun Tzu says about how to map weaknesses in competitors and take decisive action.

IDENTIFY ADVERSARIES

While Sun Tzu lived in a time where the warring entities were well identified, your battlefield is probably more nebulous. You may be in a landscape rife with mergers and acquisitions, or where one big player is crushing smaller forces. You may see new players entering your market through a revolving door, and others clandestinely rising to prominence. Identification of adversaries includes the competitors you know, and the ones you don't know.

It's a mistake to determine that you have no competitors because no one has your exact technology or processes, or because you've not done your due diligence to spot other players. Some small businesses get started and even operate for some time believing they are the only ones who can perform in a way that will satisfy the customer. It's never true. Even if you are doing something no one has ever done before, there are alternatives, even if they're less sophisticated and more costly. You must fully understand those alternatives.

CREATE OPPORTUNITIES TO DEFEAT THE ENEMY

In sparring, when you're battling someone skilled, it's not enough to stand in front of your opponent, toe-to-toe, and throw your fastest, most accurate punch or kick and expect it to land. Simple one-off blows are easily detected and deflected. That's why really good practitioners know how to use feints, counters, and multiple attacks to create opportunities and land strikes. That was a difficult lesson for me to learn in martial arts. My mentor, Uche Anusionwu, on the other hand, was quite good at it. He'd feint, I'd counter, and he'd land a blow and take me down. He would remind me yet again, usually very matter-of-factly, to "create the opening."

It's all very much the same in business, especially if you're up against a stronger adversary. You can't stand toe-to-toe, launch an attack, and expect it to land. You have to create opportunities. As he's reacting to a punch combination to the head, he's vulnerable to a knee strike or a kick in the ribs. As he blocks and turns to move out of the way of a punch, he may give you an opportunity to slip the blocking arm and slide in with a choke. The idea is to create the opening and then quickly seize the opportunity. If your opponent is skilled, he won't make the same mistake twice. And he'll be less likely to make a future mistake that would give you an opportunity.

"Create the opportunity." *Bam!* "Find the opening." *Thump!*

Taking advantage of an opening that is created by external factors is just as useful. One day, Uche and I were working on knife defense at the end of class, while the others were changing and preparing to leave. As the defender, I stood with my back to the wall, as the attacker would plunge in with the blade. Uche pulled the training knife to cut, holding it out in front, between us. Our instructor, Sensei Randy Hutchins, was standing off the mat, not really watching us. He called Uche's name to get his attention. Uche turned his head to look at Sensei. As his attention was diverted, without hesitation, I moved in, locked his wrist, threw him to the mat, and took the knife. Sensei chuckled and congratulated me. There are no rules when the bad guy has a knife.

This story illustrates a Sun Tzu principle of preparation:

Attack him where he is unprepared, appear where you are not expected.

> Take advantage of the enemy's unpreparedness, make your
> way by unexpected routes, and attack him where he has taken no
> precautions.[1]

Netflix is an excellent example of a business finding—even creating—the opening. Movie rental giant Blockbuster may have known its strengths, but it was no match for the emerging enemy, Netflix, and the innovator's ability to satisfy a market hungry for entertainment and convenience.

ENCOURAGE THE ENEMY'S MISTAKES

If you have a deep understanding of your adversary, you can play upon his weaknesses and encourage him to fall. In this passage, Sun Tzu says to exploit an adversary's ill temper:

> If your opponent is of choleric temper, seek to irritate him. Pretend
> to be weak, that he may grow arrogant.

ATTACK WEAKNESS, AVOID STRENGTH

The idea of attacking weakness and avoiding strength is central to Sun Tzu, as it must be for small businesses. Large businesses, too, would be well suited to heed this direction, but for small businesses it's mandatory.

> You may advance and be absolutely irresistible, if you make for the
> enemy's weak points; you may retire and be safe from pursuit if
> your movements are more rapid than those of the enemy.

There are two important elements here. Attack him where he is weak, never where he is strong, and do so with speed.

> When a general, unable to estimate the enemy's strength, allows
> an inferior force to engage a larger one, or hurls a weak detach-
> ment against a powerful one, and neglects to place picked soldiers
> in the front rank, the result must be rout.

You should never set the few out against the many or use weak against strong. As for leading with picked soldiers, Huang calls them "the spearhead."[2] Think of it as having all the wood behind one arrowhead so that an attack can be well coordinated, with the strongest players well positioned to maximize their potential.

MEASURE COMPETITORS

Carefully compare the opposing army with your own so that you may know where strength is abundant and where it's deficient. To reach conclusions, you'll need indicators of strength and weakness. Determine what those markers are.

> When the soldiers stand leaning on their spears, they are faint
> from want of food. If those who are sent to draw water begin by
> drinking themselves, the army is suffering from thirst.

Just as you must care for and keep the best people, you can tell a great deal about the competition from reading signs. What are your competitors lacking? Where are their frustrations? Are they experiencing significant turnover? Have their travel budgets been cut or increased? What about other spending categories? Follow your competitors' conference and trade show presence and observe their advertising spends and social media activity. These public sources can tell you where your competitors are focusing dollars, which can be an indicator of problem or plenty for them. More details on how to gain intelligence are discussed in Chapter 14, "Deception."

Be wary of adversaries who are close and quiet. Watch their movements:

> When the enemy is close at hand and remains quiet, he is relying on the natural strength of his position.

Take nothing at face value. Study your adversary's actions more than his words:

> Humble words and increased preparations are signs that the enemy is about to advance. Violent language and driving forward as if to the attack are signs that he will retreat.

TIME YOUR ATTACKS

A key piece of measuring your adversaries and attacking their weakness is the timing of attacks:

> Appear at points which the enemy must hasten to defend; march swiftly to places where you are not expected.

Agility is a primary advantage of small businesses, when contrasted with the competition. If you understand your advantages and your enemy, you'll be able to time your attacks for maximum benefit.

AVOID THE ENEMY'S TRAPS

Just as Sun Tzu recommends that his general create diversionary techniques and lure the enemy into misreading his intention, he urges that the general not fall into traps set by the competing side:

> When he [the enemy] keeps aloof and tries to provoke a battle, he is anxious for the other side to advance.
>
> If his place of encampment is easy of access, he is tendering a bait.
>
> When some are seen advancing and some retreating, it is a lure.
>
> When envoys are sent with compliments in their mouths, it is a sign that the enemy wishes for a truce.

As Huynh interprets:

> If he comes with offering, he wants rest.
>
> If the enemy's troops march up angrily and remain facing ours for a long time without either joining battle or taking themselves off again, the situation is one that demands great vigilance and circumspection.

The better you are acquainted with your adversary's design, the less likely you'll be to fall for a lure.

REMEMBER THE FORMULA

The Sun Tzu commentator, Du Mu, succinctly shares Sun Tzu's formula:

> Evade their strength, stalk their openings, and then issue a decisive attack for victory.[3]

CHOBANI

Shortly before the Greek economic crisis, my husband, Dave, and I visited Athens. It was there, in the land of the Aegean Sea, that we experienced our maiden voyage with rich, dense, and luscious Greek yogurt. We'd never tasted anything like it, and chalked it up to one more reason to go back. Imagine our joy when shortly after returning home, we found Greek yogurt popping up at all of our grocery stores.

We have Turkish immigrant Hamdi Ulukaya to thank for bringing that Mediterranean luxury to our communities. Ulukaya, the founder of Chobani, believed that Americans would like Greek yogurt, if only they had the chance to experience it. Big guys like PepsiCo, Coca-Cola, General Mills, and Kraft owned the yogurt market with products that he says are far less healthy, laden with sugar, and of a lower quality. But, said the giants, it's what the American consumer demanded.[4]

When Chobani launched in 2007, Fage, based in Greece, was exporting its yogurt to specialty stores in the U.S. and some European countries, but it was far from earning next-big-thing status. Ulukaya went to these stores and talked to Greek yogurt buyers. He and his company then tested and retested in an effort to develop a top-quality, consistent product. He didn't have any retail knowledge, but scored Chobani's first major mainstream opportunity when ShopRite agreed to let them cover shelf slotting fees with yogurt shipments instead of cash, and allowed in-store product sampling. Ulukaya convinced the grocer to put the product in the main dairy area instead of the specialty or natural section.[5] There's nothing like mainstream visibility to power a niche to explode.

In less than five years, the start-up was sharing shelf space with brand powerhouses. In a recent year, Chobani made more than

$650 million in sales and now controls about 17 percent of the U.S. yogurt market.[6] Compare that with 2007, when the Greek market share of yogurts in the United States was less than one percent.[7]

Ulukaya knew how to produce a quality product that would, in fact, appeal to the American palate and a sizable portion of consumers. But he also understood the competition. In 2009, projections indicated that Chobani should double its weekly production to 400,000 cases to meet the growing need. But not so fast. Wouldn't such a jump draw the ire of superpowers Yoplait and Dannon? Ulukaya acknowledged that risk to *Businessweek*: "For a start-up," he said, "you need to stay small so the others don't attack, or you aim to be one of the big guys. If you don't do it right, you might lose everything." Do it right, or lose everything. That's a stark dichotomy. He decided to do it right, and do it big, and positioned Chobani to exceed the projections and make 1 million cases a week. Orders rose to 1.2 million cases a week in 2011, and Chobani is branching into international sales.[8]

Chobani may have opened the floodgates to the Greek yogurt concept, but others are looking to push their way through. With competitors big and smaller coming for Chobani, we'll see if the company is able to maintain the dominant position in the Greek space.

Chobani has made many of the right moves that indicate it has knowledge of the competition, as well as the marketplace and itself. Here are some illustrations that are important themes of *The Art of War for Small Business*:

Differentiate. Without money for advertising, Ulukaya used an extra-large cup mold unlike anything else in the dairy case. He also developed unprecedented yogurt flavors like pineapple and pomegranate.[9]

Build a loyal community. Chobani used its enthusiastic customer base as the foundation of the "Chobani Love Stories" ad campaign. It let customers define what Chobani meant to them. And it doubled sales.[10] Loyalty is important, as new competitors are entering the fold and the superbrands have introduced their own Greek yogurt products, including lower-cost options.

Find a niche. "At a consumer level, the Greek yogurt trend is the biggest innovation in the dairy industry since individual packaging of things like yogurt and mozzarella sticks," Robert Ralyea, head of Cornell University's Food Processing and Development Laboratory, told Bloomberg news service. He's also credited Chobani with exceptional marketing of the innovative product.[11]

Turn disadvantage to advantage—and tell that story. "Chobani" comes from the Turkish word for *shepherd*. The company sponsored the 2012 London Olympics with superb TV advertisements that tipped the hat to its grassroots origins. Against the backdrop of the Chobani community story, the commercial tells how the product brought a revival to the local dairy farmers, plant workers, and truck drivers, and how the yogurt now powers Team USA. It featured scenes of a rural community building a makeshift theater to watch the games.[12] The ad made being the small player an advantage and forged a connection with audiences all over the country. Chobani also sponsored the U.S. Olympic team the 2014 Winter Olympics.

5

UNDERSTAND THE MARKET

Many entrepreneurs, small-business leaders, and visionaries make assumptions about the market, their customers, and their opportunities. They allow these assumptions to govern their decisions. This is the path to uninformed decision making, at best, and catastrophic decision making at worst. What assumptions are you making about your market?

> If you know the enemy and know yourself, your victory will not stand in doubt; if you know Heaven and know Earth, you may make your victory complete.

As Huang translates this Sun Tzu concept:

> By perceiving the geographical factors and perceiving the cyclic natural occurrences, victory thereby is complete.

This chapter explores marketplace factors based on the sage's analysis of ground. Sun Tzu writes extensively on types of ground, and how to plot the course based on varying circumstances. Recall Sun Tzu's five constant factors, as described in Chapter 2: Heaven can apply to weather, which we adapt to market factors and conditions that influence our maneuvers. Earth reflects the importance of maneuvering effectively and knowing the advantages and disadvantages of different types of terrain.

Sun Tzu cautions that knowledge of your organization and your adversary won't be actionable or meaningful without a complete understanding of your battlefield:

> We are not fit to lead an army on the march unless we are familiar with the face of the country—its mountains and forests, its pitfalls and precipices, its marshes and swamps.

GO WHERE THE OPPORTUNITY IS, BUT THE ENEMY IS NOT

> An army may march great distances without distress, if it marches through country where the enemy is not.

Not surprisingly, Sun Tzu directs you to go where the enemy is not. Chobani introduced the Greek yogurt concept to the mass market of American buyers, and it was some time before the big brands followed the company to that battlefield. Samuel Adams beer pioneered an American craft beer revolution. PayPal, which you'll read more about in Chapter 12, "Adaptation," reinvented online payment as we know it today.

MOVE WHEN HE HAS LET DOWN HIS GUARD

You can move to where the enemy is, if he's not expecting you, or is not prepared for an attack:

> You can be sure of succeeding in your attacks if you only attack places which are undefended.

Netflix marched into territory that was not defended by video rental giant, Blockbuster.

USE LOCAL GUIDES

> We shall be unable to turn natural advantage to account unless we make use of local guides.

The idea of a local guide can be applied in various ways by small businesses. Jim Koch lived in the Boston area, where Samuel Adams first made inroads. Hamdi Ulukaya went out and spoke to a small number of honest-to-goodness Greek yogurt buyers. Five Guys hired senior-level professionals from competing restaurant businesses. Nolan Bushnell sent his Atari engineers out into the game field and manufacturing locations. Start-ups and small businesses can bring in consultants who possess necessary expertise or form a team of trusted advisers. How can you make use of local guides?

CHOOSING GROUND

Sun Tzu identifies nine types of ground, which are interpreted somewhat differently by various scholars and authors (as shown in the accompanying table).

> The art of war recognizes nine varieties of ground: (1) Dispersive ground; (2) facile ground; (3) contentious ground; (4) open ground; (5) ground of intersecting highways; (6) serious ground; (7) difficult ground; (8) hemmed-in ground; (9) desperate ground.

SUN TZU'S NINE TYPES OF GROUND, INTERPRETED FOUR WAYS.

GILES	HUANG	MICHAELSON	HUYNH
1. Dispersive ground	Separated zones	Dispersive ground	Dispersive ground
2. Facile ground	Susceptible zones	Frontier ground	Marginal ground
3. Contentious ground	Contended zones	Key ground	Contentious ground
4. Open ground	Dually travers-able zones	Open ground	Open ground
5. Ground of intersecting highways	Key traffic zones	Focal ground	Intersecting ground
6. Serious ground	Dominant zones	Serious ground	Critical ground
7. Difficult ground	Compartmen-talized zones	Difficult ground	Difficult ground
8. Hemmed-in ground	Surrounded zones	Encircled ground	Surrounded ground
9. Desperate ground	Lethal zones	Desperate ground	Deadly ground

Let's explore these nine types of ground, and how to navigate each.

When a chieftain is fighting in his own territory, it is dispersive ground. If you are fighting in your territory, the battle has come to you. Dispersive ground is typically not a good place for a smaller organization to find itself. This is why niches are important. Samuel Adams didn't endeavor to be the top-selling domestic beer and take on Budweiser. The mission of Five Guys restaurants isn't to crush all contenders in the fast-food industry.

Chobani has decided to up the ante and draw the attention of the biggest players, but it knows what it's up against, and its CEO believes his company is well positioned.

When you're on this ground, Sun Tzu says:

- *On dispersive ground, I would inspire my men with unity of purpose.*
- *On dispersive ground, therefore, fight not.*

When he has penetrated into hostile territory, but to no great distance, it is facile ground. Facile ground is also called marginal, susceptible, or frontier ground. In the marketplace, it can be represented by the example of attempting a concept, but withdrawing it, if it doesn't meet with success or seem destined to succeed. Five Guys restaurants attempted to introduce coffee and chicken sandwiches. Both items failed and were removed from menus.

Sun Tzu says:

- *On facile ground, I would see that there is close connection between all parts of my army.*
- *On facile ground, halt not.*

On facile ground, you should keep moving so that you won't be overwhelmed by the adversary. Jim Koch knows how to make and market good beer. But Boston Beer Company also knows that not every sudsy creation will be a hit. Over the years, the company has had dozens of beers that would never come to a head commercially. The company has accepted these losses and moved on quickly.[1]

The multinational networking equipment firm Cisco Systems has a huge range of products. But it also wants to lead in the markets where it plays. Cisco has a minimum target of 40 percent share in all markets, and it will leave a market if its share drops below 20 percent. This strategy has worked for Cisco, which maintained a 70 percent share of the networking industry for the better part of the last decade.[2]

The pressure to report quarterly revenue growth leads big businesses like Cisco to focus narrowly on winning solutions. Smaller businesses have more freedom to create viable and sustainable solutions that may not be overnight successes. But they must always keep the big picture in mind and remember that there are customers and models that aren't profitable.

Ground the possession of which imports great advantage to either side, is contentious ground. This is ground that is equally advantageous for you or your adversaries to occupy. Chances are that if it's not a crowded marketplace yet, it will soon become one. Airwalk (highlighted in the sidebar) is an example of how a very successful niche product went mainstream, but ultimately was unable to hold on.

Sun Tzu advises:

- *On contentious ground, I would hurry up my rear.*
- *On contentious ground, attack not.*

Don't attack when on contentious ground because you probably don't have an advantage in numbers or power. Instead of entering into battle with an adversary on ground that is equally advantageous, plot your course carefully.

Ground on which each side has liberty of movement is open ground. For small-business purposes, open ground is similar to contentious ground. Both Huynh and Huang, in their translations, emphasize the importance of keeping your forces together in close proximity:

- *On open ground, do not become separated.* (Huynh)
- *With dually traversable zones, do not leave gaps.* (Huang)

This is ground that others will be after. Don't allow your adversary to divide you, and be sure to focus on unity from within. Sun Tzu says:

- *On open ground, I would keep a vigilant eye on my defenses.*
- *On open ground, do not try to block the enemy's way.*

Ground which forms the key to three contiguous states, so that he who occupies it first has most of the Empire at his command, is a ground of intersecting highways. Here Sun Tzu describes how to gain control of the empire. The first mover who executes well will be entrenched. But alas, if you don't have the keys to the empire in your markets just yet, consider what Sun Tzu says of intersecting roads under his discussion of a variation of tactics:

> When in difficult country, do not encamp. In country where high roads intersect, join hands with your allies. Do not linger in dangerously isolated positions.

What does it mean to join hands with allies? As Jay Abraham notes in his marketing classic, *The Sticking Point Solution,* the iconic image of the twentieth-century entrepreneur, the self-made man or woman who relies on skill, character, and grit, needs to change with the times. The twenty-first-century small-business leader has to collaborate creatively with others. He cites Robert

Hargrove's projection that the most defining characteristic of great entrepreneurs of this century will be how well they creatively collaborate with others.[3] Not one of us—not you, not me, not the brilliant entrepreneur who has five mansions on as many continents—can build all the skills necessary to keep up and compete today. Yet still, many business leaders operate like they can.

Sun Tzu says:

- *On the ground of intersecting highways, join hands with your allies.*
- *When there are means of communication on all four sides, the ground is one of intersecting highways.*
- *I would consolidate my alliances.*

You'll read more about how to join hands with allies, including in some unexpected ways, in Chapter 6, "Sun Tzu for Customers and Business Alliances."

When an army has penetrated into the heart of a hostile country, leaving a number of fortified cities in its rear, it is serious ground. Unlike facile ground, serious ground requires a deep commitment:

> When you penetrate deeply into a country, it is serious ground.
> When you penetrate but a little way, it is facile ground.

Chobani has successfully made its way to the heart of the yogurt market. But it didn't do so with just another yogurt. The company created something altogether different, and of high quality, and packaged it effectively.

Serious ground requires resources:

On serious ground, I would try to ensure a continuous stream of supplies.

And, says Sun Tzu, you should gather resources as quickly and efficiently as you can, and make the most of them:

On serious ground, gather in plunder. In difficult ground, keep steadily on the march.

Mountain forests, rugged steeps, marshes and fens—all country that is hard to traverse: this is difficult ground. Entrepreneurs in countries like Lebanon, Indonesia, and Senegal are on difficult ground. While there is a swelling spirit of innovation in these regions, young creators face traditions and cultures that are averse to innovation. Apart from the threat of competition, they must travel over very difficult terrain to achieve success. But there is big reward for making the trek. The Arabic-language portal Maktoob.com was bought by Yahoo for $175 million. Yahoo has 20 million users in the Middle East.[4]

Sun Tzu says:

- *In difficult ground, keep steadily on the march.*
- *On difficult ground, I would keep pushing on along the road.*

Entrepreneurs in the Middle East, North Africa, and sections of Asia must continue to march, even in the face of extremely difficult terrain.

Ground which is reached through narrow gorges, and from which we can only retire by tortuous paths, so that a small number of the enemy would suffice to crush a large body of our men: this is hemmed-in ground. Sun Tzu continues his description, advising that:

> When you have the enemy's strongholds on your rear, and narrow passes in front, it is hemmed-in ground.

Hemmed-in ground, also called encircled or surrounded ground, is a good place for small businesses to find a big-business adversary. On this ground a smaller force can do maximum damage. Sun Tzu advises that:

- *In hemmed-in situations, you must resort to stratagem.*
- *On hemmed-in ground, I would block any way of retreat.*

A stratagem is an artifice or trick in war used to outwit the enemy. As for blocking retreat, Sun Tzu directs his general to unite his forces so that they may not be further weakened by defectors. Blockbuster is a classic example of a business hemming itself in with a traditional model. When Netflix and other streaming video services came along with a far superior delivery mechanism, the few crushed the giant.

Ground on which we can only be saved from destruction by fighting without delay, is desperate ground. This situation differs from hemmed-in ground, which allows "narrow passes in front." With desperate ground, however, there is no place of refuge at all. The situation is dire, indeed:

> On desperate ground, I would proclaim to my soldiers the hopelessness of saving their lives.

There is one option, says Sun Tzu:

On desperate ground, fight.

Priceline, which is profiled in "Perseverance" and mentioned again in "Adaptation" (Chapters 8 and 12, respectively), is an example of a company on desperate ground that was turned from despair to advantage.

———

For small businesses, all ground can be difficult. On intersection grounds, you need to depend on partners and friends. When isolated and open, take cover or move. When surrounded, you need strategy. When you have no choice, fight.

If you have a viable concept, you'll only be left alone for a short time. Many small businesses opt to go to surrounded ground, where there is tremendous opportunity but also lots of competition. If you do that, you'll need ample strength to handle the challenges that will come. Remember that on surrounded ground, a few of them, positioned well, can attack and defeat many of you. But, if you are able to take the superior position and surround your competitor(s), few of you can defeat many of them.

DON'T FOLLOW A PREPARED ADVERSARY

In one more warning from Sun Tzu, be sure not to follow a prepared adversary into his market:

> If the enemy occupies [narrow ground] first, and is prepared, do not follow him. If he is not prepared, follow him.[5]

This passage, from Sun Tzu's nines types of terrain, speaks of a narrow pass where maneuvering is difficult. The application for small businesses is to avoid a strong competitor's well-guarded, highly satisfied, difficult-to-tap customers when the passage is narrow. Competitive markets equate to narrow passes. It's the unprepared adversary, particularly one without a firm hold on customers, that you want to pursue.

KNOW WHEN TO PIVOT

As we'll see in the chapter on adaptation, sometimes the solution isn't to despair or to crumble, but to change your business model and overcome. Many businesses have seen victory by calculating and taking a new route.

AIRWALK

One of my favorite examples of a business going to extraordinary lengths to understand its market and position itself most advantageously is Airwalk. The athletic shoe company was founded in the mid-1980s with a focus on serious skateboarders. Airwalk developed a passionate cult following, and, after a few short years, it was a $13-million-a-year business. The owners next sought to build this small business into an international brand. They branched out into surfing, snowboarding, mountain biking, and bicycle racing. They also hired a small ad agency, Lambesis. Within two years, Airwalk was huge.

With a limited budget, Lambesis came up with a series of outstanding images showing people relating to their Airwalks, followed by very memorable TV commercials. The ads were stunningly visual and made powerful appeals to youth. But if they were going to make Airwalk into a huge brand, they had to do something more. They had to capture the trendsetting skateboarding subculture and package it for mass consumption.[6]

To uncover these ideas, Lambesis developed a network of savvy young people in major international cities and put together a picture of evolving new trends. By comparing its findings with what the mainstream kids were saying and doing, Lambesis could track the ideas that were likely to make the jump from the cool subculture to the mainstream. These ideas would become integral to the Lambesis ads and the Airwalk brand.[7]

What the team was able to do is extraordinary. They picked up on nascent trends and created ads to showcase and translate them so that they made sense. By the time the ads ran, those trends (or at least many of them) had hit. For example, the subculture was into kung fu movies. So Lambesis made a kung fu parody ad where the Airwalk hero fights off villains with, what else? His skateboard. Lambesis took the kung fu idea and mashed it up with youth culture.

But unfortunately for Airwalk, the company's story also illustrates how not to apply Sun Tzu effectively because it failed to heed this principle:

> If we know that the enemy is open to attack, but are unaware that our own men are not in a condition to attack, we have gone only halfway towards victory.

The market was open to Airwalk. But the brand moved its forces out of position to continue to attack and dominate. While they demonstrated a profound understanding of the customer, they didn't sustain it. Following their peak in the mid-1990s, Airwalk experienced production problems. Distributors, once so loyal, lost patience.[8]

As another illustration of the company not being in a condition to attack, Airwalk also lost focus on its cutting-edge feel. The product became less cool. It was no longer a shoe for innovative performers. Airwalk even moved away from their strategy of giving small independent skate shops an exclusive product line of more technical shoes that weren't available elsewhere. At one time the trendsetters could wear a better, more exclusive shoe than everyone else. But then, Airwalk dropped this niche strategy and offered up the same shoes to mass malls.[9]

PAYCHEX

If your small business uses a payroll-processing service, there's a good chance it's Paychex. The company illustrates the power of understanding the market well enough to find the opening and create opportunity.

In 1971, Tom Golisano saw the potential in bringing affordable payroll outsourcing to businesses with fewer than 100 employees. Industry heavyweight ADP focused on businesses with more employees. With only 5 percent of its revenue from smaller employers, ADP continued to maintain its target of larger customers. Golisano went to his employer at the time, a regional payroll processor for big businesses, with his plan. The company wasn't interested, so he started Paychex.[10]

Paychex went where the competition had not prepared to go, and didn't want to go. Since then, Paychex has had a record of steady growth. As currently reported on the Paychex corporate website, in fiscal 2013, the company reported revenues exceeding $2.3 billion. Growing from just one employee, Paychex has more than 12,000 employees and serves half a million small to medium-size businesses nationwide.

6

SUN TZU FOR CUSTOMERS AND BUSINESS ALLIANCES

With the Internet connecting us all together, companies are becoming more and more transparent, whether they embrace it or are being dragged to interconnected utopia kicking and screaming. A single unhappy customer or disgruntled employee can share one bad experience with the world in about as much time as it took you to read this sentence. Their story, which may be true, false, or somewhere in between, can spread like wildfire via social networks.

The good news is that the reverse is true as well. A great experience with a company can be read by millions of people almost instantaneously.

Social media gives small businesses unprecedented power to understand and engage with customers and the rest of their community. And there's something else that's equally exciting: If you build a small company that demonstrates a desire to engage with influencers, they'll want to connect with you—much more so than they will the big corporate brands. Then, when you become a big brand, you can solve the enviable problem of how to stay dynamic and engagement-worthy, while also counting your billions. Zappos has figured out how to use social media to this very end.

We've explored Sun Tzu's direction on knowing the enemy and ourselves. In this chapter, we'll extend Sun Tzu's vision for allies and stakeholders, including customers. Maximizing relationships and value from customers, partners, suppliers, and other influencers is a major strategic consideration.

Sun Tzu wrote of stakeholders and assets, including spies, local guides, and defeated forces within enemy ranks. He understood the need to influence combatants and noncombatants alike, but he didn't have to contend with a dynamic like the customer. We do, however. And we can gain insight from him about how to optimize all of our business relationships.

CUSTOMERS

Salesforce.com CEO and enthusiastic *Art of War* pupil Marc Benioff has said that there is one commitment that all successful salespeople and marketers share. That's a "relentless focus on the customer and a real commitment to his or her success." The entire organization must pursue this mantra.[1]

Small businesses, in particular, should extend Sun Tzu's call for deep knowledge of ourselves and our adversaries to deep knowledge and commitment to the customer. The mandate for providing exceptional customer care is the sea change differentiator for small businesses competing against large "faceless brands." Renowned branding consultant and author Joe Calloway has three rules for developing an intimate relationship with the customer, rules that would make Sun Tzu proud:

1. Know more about the customer than anyone else.
2. Get closer to the customer than anyone else.
3. Emotionally connect with the customer better than anyone else.[2]

They're simple, but these three rules separate exceptional businesses from all others. James Beard, the namesake of the culinary James Beard awards, put it best when he was asked to divulge his favorite restaurant. Everyone who cares about developing outstanding customer relationships should listen to his response: "My favorite restaurant is where they know me; they treat me like a family member and a friend."

This level of intimacy is so important that Beard said that even if the food isn't quite as good at the place where they know him best, he would still prefer to eat there and spend his money there. It's the same with restaurants and hotels.[3]

Small businesses are uniquely capable of getting to know the customer extremely well. Atari's decision to have its engineers visit test locations moved these developers much closer to the customer. It also gave the video game developer rapid feedback on game popularity. All they had to do was count quarters. They could test the market and predict earnings for new games, and give distributors an informed idea of what to expect.[4] Are you as close to your customers as you could be? Do you know them as well as you could?

ALLIES

We're well into the era of alliances. Strategic alliances are on the upswing for large organizations. Management guru Peter Drucker has noted that we're in the midst of "a worldwide restructuring" taking place in the shape of alliances and partnerships.[5] And if the biggest businesses are pulling resources with other high rollers, how much more do small businesses need to build strong alliances and relationships?

Too many people think very narrowly about strategic alliances. They think only about what a potential partner can do for them in the short term. If they can't come up with a home run, then they dismiss that opportunity. Instead, small businesses must think strategically about building alliances with the right organizations to gain an advantage that benefits both parties. Small businesses should actively and carefully seek allies, including with vendors and suppliers, peer companies, strategic partners, joint venture partners, funders, go-to consultants, colleagues, and friends. Successful small businesses must think in terms of collaboration, today more than ever. The more resources you have, the greater your footprint.

While still at eBay, Meg Whitman noted this cooperative alliance shift. Speaking to *Financial Times,* she remembers earlier in her career that teaming with a competitor was taboo. Hasbro never worked with rival toymaker Mattel. Procter & Gamble didn't cooperate with Colgate. But, she noted of eBay's partnership with Yahoo, it's all changed. Google, too, was an eBay partner, as well as a competitor.[6] Alliances are important to Sun Tzu, as they are for all shrewd business and military leaders. Disruption of the adversary's alliances, too, is a worthwhile pursuit:

> The supreme excellence in war is to attack the enemy's plans. Next best is to disrupt his alliances. The next best is to attack his army. The worst policy is to attack cities.[7]

Allies Can Help Close the Gap

> If you are situated at a great distance from the enemy, and the strength of the two armies is equal, it is not easy to provoke a battle, and fighting will be to your disadvantage.

While this passage refers to evenly matched adversaries, it's important for small businesses. If you have to fight hard to get to the customer base in an industry, you'll be at a disadvantage. How you can you make the fight lighter and more easily shore up the gap? Sun Tzu says to engage with superior, not equal, strength. By leveraging carefully picked allies, you can help close the chasm between your small business and the bigger ones you seek to dominate.

Carefully Consider Alliances

Regardless of the specific nature of the business agreement, alliances shouldn't be entered into lightly. Deep understanding of potential partners is required by Sun Tzu:

> We cannot enter into alliances until we are acquainted with the designs of our neighbors.

Alliances require due diligence to guard against conflicts of interest and damage to your reputation and bottom line. Small businesses can easily fall victim to the trap of gathering as many strategic alliances as they can, but never really understanding how best to leverage these partnerships. I worked with a company in the telecom space when the dotcom bubble exploded, to the chagrin of so many of us. This reasonably well-funded company had a plethora of signed agreements of strategic alliances but never really did much with these "partners" outside of collecting signatures on papers. Unable to make substantive sales, the company ran out of cash and closed up shop. Its partners were either poorly educated about how to promote the telecom service provider's wares, or poorly incentivized, or both.

The smart general, Sun Tzu writes, "does not strive to ally himself with all and sundry." If the alliance isn't designed to play a role in generating revenue, it's probably a waste of time.

Instead, smart business leaders develop clear objectives with all of their partners. An objective can be to better understand a new territory:

> We shall be unable to turn natural advantages to account unless we make use of local guides.

How can you make use of "local guides" when you seek to become "acquainted with the designs of [your] neighbors"? If you are entering into a new market or region, you'll need a guide who understands this landscape better than you do, whether it's on the employee side or the consultant side. The consulting model works well for many small businesses, but consultants naturally lack the loyalty and are typically less vested than employees. No matter what your resources, if you are using the same local guides as your competitors, are you really getting ahead?

BOURBON INDUSTRY

One of my favorite examples of Sun Tzu's direction to "join hands with your allies" while on intersecting ground is seen in the bourbon industry. When my husband and I toured the Kentucky

Bourbon Trail®, we were struck by the spirit of community among the different distilleries. The Bourbon Trail features eight major distilleries, and has since added a Craft Tour to highlight smaller bourbon producers. No one had an unkind word to say about any other distiller, though you should be ready for some good-natured heckling if, for example, you go to Buffalo Trace wearing a Maker's Mark T-shirt.

Bourbon has been booming in recent years. We were in good company at the distilleries we visited, on and off the trail. In 2012, more than half a million people visited one or more distilleries in Kentucky, the state where 95 percent of the country's bourbon is produced. Bourbon generated $4.5 billion in retail sales in 2012.[8]

The family tradition of Kentucky bourbon runs deeply in the lime-rich water of the Kentucky River. The Jim Beam family has had a hand in just about every major distillery in the state. The family connection flowing through so many generations of bourbon distilling is a contributing factor to, well, the spirit behind the whiskey.

But before bourbon became a billion-dollar industry, it faced some tough times. It had been declining since the early 1970s, as drinkers preferred more neutral gins and vodkas. In 1984, renowned distiller Elmer T. Lee produced the first batch of Blanton's Single Barrel. He had nothing to lose, but as a chorus of bourbon aficionados will tell you, we had so very much to gain. Buffalo Trace, where the late Elmer Lee served as master distiller, sold this premium bourbon for $30 a bottle, two to three times as much as average prices of other bourbons at that time.[9]

Slowly, Blanton's Single Barrel built loyal customers. Today, many Kentucky distilleries offer premium products. They have Lee to thank. His innovation architected the turnaround that has charted the course to this explosion in premium bourbons.[10] And it's met with solid market demand.

The reasons for these strong alliances among bourbon makers can probably be seen both in the familial ties of the generations who produce it, as well as the need to band together to protect interests from threats posed by taxes and trade barriers. And perhaps collectively they see gins, vodkas, and other concoctions as competitors that they need to band together to fight.

Alliance Building for Your Small Business

Here are some powerful alliance-building tips and examples you can use to build your small business.

Marketing strategist and author Jay Abraham suggests sharing resources. If you need a sales force, but your young or struggling business can't afford it, find a noncompeting partner in your field who has a force that isn't being fully utilized, set up a joint venture (JV), and share in the profits. If you need a warehouse, find a business with extra storage space or delivery capacity, and do a JV to share in the growth.[11]

Bartering, too, can be a boon to your business, although it is often viewed with skepticism. After all, it's about making money, not breaking even, right? Not so fast. Consider an experience Abraham had. He worked with the number three travel market magazine publisher that was struggling to sell ads in any sort of predicable way. The publisher had offers from businesses to barter, but it turned them down. But Abraham and his team converted those barters to cash at 50 cents on the dollar. This equated to five times the ad cost. The magazine was able to trade ad space for goods or service worth $10,000 per page to businesses happy to pay 50 cents on the dollar for the exposure.[12]

In another bartering success story, Carnival Cruise Lines started out trading otherwise empty cabins for radio, TV, and newspaper advertising. What it got in return was continuous advertising in a hundred cities over a period of more than ten years. Plus, these media passengers spent a healthy amount at the bar, casino, and gift shop. Abraham conservatively estimates the amount of sales in the hundreds of millions of dollars. The owner became a billionaire and one of Forbes Richest People in America.[13]

That's the power of bartering! It takes vision and creativity, but it can pay off in very big ways.

Work Your Network

Ultimately, your success hinges on who you know. If you are not out there talking to potential customers and industry experts, you'll miss out on countless opportunities. Think about how you can build a powerful network.

Pete's Greens is a certified organic, four season vegetable farm in Craftsbury, Vermont. Company president Pete Johnson was involved in a business owners group that met regularly for potlucks. At each meeting, they would discuss a topic that one of the members was struggling with. That was a creative way to introduce solutions and shape networks.[14]

EBAY

Alliances were at the heart of Meg Whitman's strategy at eBay. In *Sun Tzu for Women*, I wrote of Whitman's incredible ability to build partnerships and alliances. She went to eBay's channel partners to learn how the company could enhance their businesses, which is credited as a driving factor behind the success of the online auction house. Called the chief executive enabler because of the outstanding teams she built, Whitman is a case study in Sun Tzu for customers, employees, and alliances. When she joined eBay in 1998, it had thirty employees and approximately $4 million in revenue. Ten years later, she left a publicly traded global powerhouse boasting $8 billion in revenue. Now, it remains to be seen how she'll translate past performance into a channel partner strategy at HP.

DENNIS PUBLISHING

HP has a wealth of resources. But when I think of how entrepreneurs with very few resources can apply their savvy to build partnerships and alliances to catapult them forward, I think of Felix Dennis. He owns Dennis Publishing and its more than fifty magazine titles, websites, and mobile sites. One of the wealthiest men in England, he's built an $800 million publishing empire.[15]

But in 1972, Dennis had nothing but ideas. The story behind the early days of his success is a testament to the power of partnerships. He was either persuasive, pitiful, or incorrigible, or perhaps all three. Dennis sought to start a comic book company. With little money, he hired a close friend, Dick Pountain, to be codirector and production manager. They found undesirable but useful office space whose previous occupants included notorious heavy metal legend Lemmy Kilmister from Motörhead and a puppy breeding operation. He persuaded a young lawyer named Bernie Simons to help him register his LLC. He paid Simons a small nominal fee for his services. Dennis said he "amused" a bank manager enough to open a company account. A magazine distributor he'd known agreed to carry his first product, though Dennis had no money to exchange for it. As for content, he and Dick knew illustrators who wouldn't expect to be paid in advance, or at all, for their efforts.[16]

Printing was an expensive and formidable obstacle. Dennis persuaded a printer to provide machine time and paper to produce the comic, substantially reducing the costs to a few thousand dollars. But the printers needed some guarantee that they would be paid. Dennis persuaded (there's that word again) the owners of his potential comic distributors to write to the printer and promise the money. They knew better than to offer a legal guarantee, but they made it sound convincing. The distributor he engaged had considerable clout in the industry. The printer agreed.[17]

The first issue of *Cozmic Comics* barely made a cent, but it provided a framework for more publishing ventures. Within two years, our hero had the equivalent of roughly US$800 million by today's standard. He was able to pay his printers, contributors, designers, landlord, attorney, Dick—and himself—as he retained complete control of the company. All these people who helped him during those formative months were instrumental. Without them, he recognizes, he never could have done it.[18]

Dennis's advice is that you may be surprised at how many people will want to help you. And, in Sun Tzu fashion, the people who helped him were well cared for, from the young lawyer who would later establish the law firm that would represent Dennis throughout his career, to the printer who continued to print for him, at least until the date of his autobiography. Yes, in the end, they made out just fine.[19]

His story also illustrates another Sun Tzu principle that's useful for small businesses: *Make forays in fertile country in order to supply your army with food.* The initial printing of that comic book was like a quick, sudden raid or attack that supplied the growing business with the bare minimums it needed to keep moving. From there it grew and grew. Like Dennis and Sun Tzu, even as you are envisioning how you'll build your empire, remember that you need to feed the beast.

The Defeated Enemy Is the New Ally

In a continuation of Sun Tzu's direction on capturing chariots (see Chapter 3, "Understand Yourself"), he says:

> Our own flags should be substituted for those of the enemy, and the chariots mingled and used in conjunction with ours. The captured soldiers should be kindly treated and kept.

This direction on how to care humanely for captured soldiers may strike some as unexpected from a career warrior. But consider how relevant this advice is for business. We've all seen our share of proverbial bridges get burned. Maybe we were the ones holding the torch or left stranded in hostile territory. Regardless, we've seen enemies made. Apart from a short-term ego boost, what good does it do to wrong others or deal hostilely with them?

Vengeance may feel good in the short term, but beware if you spend your career in a single industry or the same town, even if it's a big city. The bridges you burn will one day cut you off. It's a brutal world. Small-business leaders need all the friends we can get.

When you overtake competitors, or acquire them, consider how you'll treat those new employees. Sometimes carnage ensues. But remember that these performers can be sources of intellectual property and informal information. Think about how proper treatment of top talent will benefit your business, as well as the damage they may do to you by going to your competition.

For competitors who aren't doing very well, consider a friendly takeover. You can acquire their customers and allow your competitor to save face. It's a comparatively low-cost, high-impact way for you to grow your business.

SUPPLIERS AND DISTRIBUTORS

Small businesses should maximize the value of their supplier and distributor relationships. These are often underappreciated and underutilized. For small businesses, cash flow is king. When needed, creatively work with these partners to help keep the cash flowing. Also, the better you know them, the better you can leverage them against one another for your maximum gain. But don't be abusive or dishonest. Suppliers have important competitive and market information. Treat them well. Build their trust. Make it a point to meet with key suppliers and distributors over lunch or drinks so that you can ferret out information.

Humility is an attribute for small-business leaders. Video game innovator Atari had serious cash flow problems in the early days, as the company was still building traction. Cofounder Nolan Bushnell was running out of options. He turned to what he calls "a community of help." He went to microprocessor producer AMD. He owed this supplier for parts shipped more than ninety days previously, but he told them he still needed more parts. He explained how he could pay for all of the parts once he got Atari over an imminent hurdle. AMD consented, and that solidified a relationship that would lead to many large future orders for the microprocessor. It worked out well for Atari, too. They sold millions of gaming consoles and computers and became the fastest-growing company in the history of the United States up until that point.[20]

Even consider your customers when you need help. Jeff Hoffman, founder and former CEO of Priceline, suggests turning to your customers for help when you're stuck, or even when you're desperate. Tell them you want to do something or build something, explain how it will benefit them, and tell them how they can help you.[21] For this approach to work, you have to have a good relationship with your customers, and they have to trust you.

The motivation and character of leadership, which will be covered extensively in the next chapter, "Embody the General," is precious to Sun Tzu. The best leaders seek the best interests of the people who contribute to their successes, from employees and customers to all variety of partners.

PART THREE

PRINCIPLES FOR
THE
BATTLEFIELD

The four chapters in this part build from the essentials of understanding into progressively more advanced Sun Tzu. Here we'll focus on the character necessary to be a successful small-business leader and practitioner, so you can internalize many of Sun Tzu's principles and apply them. This material presents an intermediate level of understanding Sun Tzu for small business.

7

EMBODY THE GENERAL

Sun Tzu is often studied in the context of leadership, and for good reason. He calls for his general to have such attributes as boldness, decisiveness, foresight, disciplined organization, resource stewardship, and sensitivity to the army. This extends to proper care of defeated armies, as we saw in the previous chapter. Sun Tzu is not singularly concerned with winning the battles that are before him. Like you, he's concerned with the long game.

Sun Tzu offers much for leaders seeking to overcome the challenges that many small businesses succumb to, such as failing to consolidate gains, losing focus, allowing fragmentation to occur within the ranks, and mismanaging resources. It's only from behind a strong leader that a small business can execute on its grand strategy.

The word for "general," translated as *j-iang,* means head of the army. It also means an official position like a civilian governor or district chief. Sun Tzu's *j-iang* was a civilian administrator of both people and military affairs. The term roughly corresponds to a proconsul of the Roman Empire. While there's not a precise English equivalent, Huang says "general" is a loose interpretation.[1] Sun Tzu said:

> The Commander stands for the virtues of wisdom, sincerity, benevolence, courage, and strictness.

We explore Sun Tzu based on those virtues.

VIRTUE 1: WISDOM

Sun Tzu's direction on wisdom for the leader is extensive and meaningful. Are you following these principles?

Maximize Resources

> The skillful leader subdues the enemy's troops without any fighting; he captures their cities without laying siege to them; he overthrows their kingdom without lengthy operations in the field.

The wise general aspires to win without fighting. This is an important theme of *The Art of War*, and one that probably defies preconceived notions about a book on military strategy. How do you defeat the enemy without fighting? The answer is in making the absolute best use of the resources within your organization to defeat the bigger budgets of your adversaries. If possible, you can buy the competition. You can innovate to take their customers, without a messy battle. Use better suppliers, and use them exclusively. Find better, cheaper ways to get your product to market.

Hire better people and keep them longer. Create ecstatic customers who won't be wooed away by your competitors.

Always seek to choose the strategy most in line with Sun Tzu's counsel, and make the most of your small business's limited resources. Small businesses have unprecedented access to low-cost advertising and marketing options that can generate huge returns on investment for those that use them wisely. Social media has far-reaching influence over consumers' purchasing decisions. As with all initiatives, if you use these resources, be sure that they are integrated into the overall strategic plan so that all the wood is behind one arrowhead.

Also, when it comes to maximizing resources, don't make the common mistake of being so consumed with acquisition of new customers that you lose sight of the criticality of fully leveraging your present and past customers. This costly and foolish oversight happens too commonly, and small businesses looking to overtake all comers can't afford to make this mistake and sacrifice any traction they've gained.

Making wise use of resources is fundamental:

> Hence the saying: The enlightened ruler lays his plans well ahead; the good general cultivates his resources.

Wise leaders don't allow their smaller, weaker forces to fight toe-to-toe with large armies:

> When a general, unable to estimate the enemy's strength, allows an inferior force to engage a larger one, or hurls a weak detachment against a powerful one, and neglects to place picked soldiers in the front rank, the result must be rout.

Provide the Right Resources

Employees at small businesses have to be willing to make the best of limited resources. Larger counterparts have more sophisticated enterprise software tools and other infrastructure. Despite being a smaller player, it's essential that small-business leaders give their teams the resources they need to be successful, even if it's the cost-effective yet sometimes cumbersome minivan instead of the hotshot's shiny new sports car. And leaders have to listen to their people when they tell them what they need. Sun Tzu said there are three ways "a ruler can bring misfortune upon his army." One of them is:

> By commanding the army to advance or to retreat, being ignorant of the fact that it cannot obey. This is called hobbling the army.

Your organization must have the resources necessary to do what its leaders ask it to do.

Devise Unfathomable Plans

We examined Sun Tzu's direction on how you should treat employees in Chapter 3, "Understand Yourself." The strong leader wisely uses resources to ensure her people aren't asked to do more than is manageable. Instead, she stores up strength so that these resources can be utilized most effectively. In this way, she's able to develop schemes that the competition does not and cannot grasp:

> Carefully study the well-being of your men, and do not overtax them. Concentrate your energy and hoard your strength. Keep

your army continually on the move, and devise unfathomable plans.

Leverage Experience

Wisdom is gained through experience:

> It is only one who is thoroughly acquainted with the evils of war that can thoroughly understand the profitable way of carrying it on.

Of course, Sun Tzu's general is experienced. If you are not deeply experienced in your domain or are entering ground that is terra incognita, the solution is to work with experts who've done it before.

With experience comes perspective. The more difficult the situations you've encountered in business, the better you're able to calibrate and adapt to the next challenge.

Overcome Anger

Battle should never be fought for ego or pride. Sun Tzu's general isn't prone to anger:

> The general, unable to control his irritation, will launch his men to the assault like swarming ants, with the result that one-third of his men are slain, while the town still remains untaken. Such are the disastrous effects of a siege.
>
> Anger may in time change to gladness; vexation may be succeeded by content. But a kingdom that has once been destroyed can never come again into being; nor can the dead ever be brought back to life.

Wise leaders know their decisions have consequences and they behave accordingly. Other emotions that can be dangerous to the general are highlighted in the discussion of Virtue 5: Strictness.

Perfect Patience

While driven and capable of moving with blazing speed to reach an objective, the general has the wisdom to wait for the best opportunity to defeat the adversary:

> When, in consequence of heavy rains up-country, a river which you wish to ford is swollen and flecked with foam, you must wait until it subsides.

VIRTUE 2: SINCERITY

Leadership is serious business, indeed:

> The leader of armies is the arbiter of the people's fate, the man on whom it depends whether the nation shall be in peace or in peril.

Be Consistent

Sincere leaders are consistent. Leaders who go back and forth on decisions and priorities raise doubts among their people, yet these tendencies are all too common among many growing businesses. Honoring your word is a mark of sincerity. Some leaders lose sight of the importance of keeping commitments and doing what they say they're going to do.

When Jerry Murrell started the Five Guys burger chain, he still had a day job. Unable to get a loan from a financial institution, he turned to 100 friends and acquaintances and asked each for loans of $10,000 to $30,000. In exchange, they received high interest and Murrell's commitment to always pay them on time, each and every month.[2] Details like these are important to your small business. So are friends.

On being consistent and keeping your word, Jason Cohen, president of ILM Corporation, a data entry, scanning, indexing, document management, and clerical services small business, says: "It comes from your mother. And she says when you tell somebody you're going to do something, do it." This rule applies to employees, vendors, customers, and prospects, he says. Keep your word.[3]

Unite Them Around a Cause

The army should never question their leader's conviction. Instead, he must effectively rally the forces to his cause. For Sun Tzu, one method of unity is in the dire consequences of losing:

> Throw your soldiers into positions whence there is no escape, and they will prefer death to flight. If they will face death, there is nothing they may not achieve. Officers and men alike will put forth their uttermost strength.

In Chapter 10, we'll further explore Sun Tzu's direction on unity.

Understand the Sincerity Paradox

There's an aspect of sincerely in Sun Tzu that, at first, seems contradictory:

He must be able to mystify his officers and men by false reports and appearances, and thus keep them in total ignorance.

This challenging, even off-putting passage is from a section on changing plans and keeping the enemy from knowing your next move. Huynh explains it as the desire to prevent the soldiers from knowing the general's overall strategy. By keeping them "in total ignorance," the general insulates his soldiers from the specific troubles and complexities he faces as a leader. But it is an act of benevolence too, because it frees them to concentrate fully on their individual roles, which are essential to the prescribed execution. Think about how insulating your people from high-level burdens will positively impact their performance. Keep them from being taxed by matters they don't need to be concerned with, or that will only confuse them, hinder them, or drain morale.[4]

Huang explains that our modern understanding of this impetus to keep warriors and soldiers figuratively in the dark represents a gap in meaning. It is not to "fool" them, but requires a complete calibration of action, he believes.[5]

While Guidewire Software CEO Marcus Ryu hasn't suggested deceiving his people, he has noted a communications dynamic that sheds light on this aspect of Sun Tzu. As he noted in a *New York Times* interview, when you are communicating to a large number of people, even very smart people, they tend to appear to get "dumber" in a larger collective group. With a larger audience, the message has to be simple and brief, Ryu said.[6]

VIRTUE 3: BENEVOLENCE

Far from a warmonger, Sun Tzu calls his general to be governed by justice:

It is the business of a general to be quiet and thus ensure secrecy; upright and just, and thus maintain order.

In a demonstration of benevolence that also benefits the general, Sun Tzu urges care for captured soldiers:

The captured soldiers should be kindly treated and kept.

Similarly, your competitors' employees, past and present, could have some value for you.

The people in the trenches who make success happen must be rewarded:

Now in order to kill the enemy, our men must be roused to anger; that there may be advantage from defeating the enemy, they must have their rewards.

Strictness is important for Sun Tzu, but note that discipline is coupled with humanity in this passage. Leaders are smart to remember this order:

Soldiers must be treated in the first instance with humanity, but kept under control by means of iron discipline. This is a certain road to victory.

Check Your Motivations

Sun Tzu acknowledges that "war is a costly endeavor." The benevolent general maintains a healthy perspective that is larger than he is:

To be parsimonious with positions, compensations, or hundreds of
pounds of gold, and thereby blind to the enemy's status, is to be
extraordinarily inhumane.[7]

Leaders shouldn't let their concerns for personal gains cloud
their duty to perceive the enemy. As we'll read in the "Deception"
chapter, spies, too, aren't to be used for personal greed, but to
advance the army's strategic objectives.

VIRTUE 4: COURAGE

Strong leaders have enough courage to set and keep their people
focused on the goal. They're able to harness the power of their
teams to enable decisive victory.

Maximize Energy

As discussed already, maximizing resources and providing your
team with needed tools, processes, and infrastructure are necessary for a small business to succeed. Extending this idea further,
the extraordinary general makes the absolute most of the energy
of his forces. Here's what Sun Tzu says about this important concept:

The clever combatant looks to the effect of combined energy, and
does not require too much from individuals. Hence his ability to
pick out the right men and utilize combined energy.

Timing and decisiveness are essential for maximizing energy:

Energy may be likened to the bending of a crossbow; decision, to the releasing of a trigger.

The question for the leader is, how are you setting the crossbow and making powerful decisions that equate to the release of a trigger?

Sound decisions acted on decisively lead to more rapid victory, which is important to small businesses that need to husband their resources:

In war, then, let your great object be victory, not lengthy campaigns.

Successful leaders make decisions and conduct operations by asking: Will this action further our objectives? If so, how? Will it make us money? It the activity isn't tied to winning, the leader doesn't pursue it. He keeps everyone unified by the same objectives and goals:

When the men are united, the brave cannot advance alone, the cowardly cannot retreat alone. These are the principles for employing a large number of troops.[8]

VIRTUE 5: STRICTNESS

Sun Tzu has much to say about the disciplines necessary for an army to meet with success. Controlling a large army requires adherence to the same principles as does controlling a small force.

Hierarchy

Hierarchy and structure are fundamental components of strictness.

> By method and discipline are to be understood the marshaling of the army in its proper subdivisions, the graduations of rank among the officers, the maintenance of roads by which supplies may reach the army, and the control of military expenditure.

This is how even a large force is led.

> The control of a large force is the same principle as the control of a few men: it is merely a question of dividing up their numbers.

Traits of hierarchy and consistency are evident in this passage:

> When the general is weak and without authority; when his orders are not clear and distinct; when there are no fixed duties assigned to officers and men, and the ranks are formed in a slovenly haphazard manner, the result is utter disorganization.

This, too, tells us of the importance of consistency and clarity if the people are to respond to direction in a predictable and effective manner:

> If in training soldiers commands are habitually enforced, the army will be well disciplined; if not, its discipline will be bad.

If small businesses are to take advantage of their competitive advantages, orders and roles must be clear. But leaders should never confuse openness, transparency, and collaboration with an ineffectual flat structure that entails slow decisions and a weak and nebulous chain of command.

Five Dangerous Faults

Sun Tzu tells us of the five dangerous faults that can hinder a general:

1) Recklessness, which leads to destruction

2) Cowardice, which leads to capture

3) A hasty temper, which can be provoked by insults

4) A delicacy of honor which is sensitive to shame

5) Over-solicitude for his men, which exposes him to worry and trouble

These are the five besetting sins of a general, ruinous to the conduct of war.

If you're reckless, you'll make mistakes, just like the ones you want the enemy to make. If you're a coward, good people will not trust you or work with or for you. A short fuse causes mistakes and doing battle for the wrong reason. A delicacy of honor will also lead you to fight the wrong battles for the wrong reasons. Excessive sensitivity to the people who work with you will prevent you from leading them and making the tough decisions.

Despite the difficult and bloody business of leading troops into battle, Sun Tzu puts the role of the general, and the enlightened ruler, into perspective. This passage comes at the end of a chapter on how to attack and destroy with fire, imparting to us Sun Tzu's wise perspective:

The enlightened ruler is heedful, and the good general full of caution. This is the way to keep a country at peace and an army intact.

Perhaps the most telling of all of Sun Tzu's observations about the character of a general is this sentence, which we'll use to conclude this chapter:

> The general who advances without coveting fame and retreats without fearing disgrace, whose only thought is to protect his country and do good service for his sovereign, is the jewel of the kingdom.

8

PERSEVERANCE

Entrepreneurs know what it means to fail. But the ones who succeed are the ones who persevere to win the next battles. The people who lead small businesses must endure many challenges, and they must stare down and overcome defeat. Perseverance, of course, is a primary differentiator between the successful small businesses and everybody else. It's also integral to Sun Tzu.

For the sage, even the most disadvantaged army can be successful with the right spirit. He directs us to turn disadvantage to advantage and miss no opportunity to defeat the enemy. When difficulties come, small businesses don't have the resources to wait it out. We must take action, and are well advised to follow the principles of Sun Tzu.

Perseverance has been the watchword of entrepreneurs since people first decided they were going to find or build something, and then sell it. The success literature starting in the first half of the twentieth century is all about stick-to-itiveness. No study of

Sun Tzu, or of small-business champions, is served without an examination of perseverance.

Noah Thomas Leask, president and CEO of ISHP, an information technology firm that serves the cybersecurity and defense sector, put it this way: "Do not underestimate the amount of effort, perseverance, and discipline that is required to be successful. I cannot stress that enough. There will be problems and you must be ready mentally, physically, and spiritually to deal with them. If you are starting a business to get rich and work less, then you are on the wrong path. One should be working on enjoying the journey, not thinking about the destination. The riches-seekers never reach it."[1]

Leask's characterization is similar here to Sun Tzu's precious "jewel of the kingdom," described in the previous chapter.

READINESS TO SEIZE ADVANTAGES

Here is one of my favorite passages from Sun Tzu, and I believe it's one that all small business warriors should have etched in their psyche:

> If, on the other hand, in the midst of difficulties we are always ready to seize an advantage, we may extricate ourselves from misfortune.

We should always be prepared to extract victory from defeat, and be prepared to weather misfortune. The people behind mall businesses understand adversity. They are used to the odds being stacked against them. But beyond that, you need to be ready for the unexpected so that your team can turn disadvantage to advantage. A difficult economy provides a good example of this principle. If your competitors are struggling, they may cut corners; go for short-term gains at the expense of long-term profit; make rash, reactionary decisions; and lose sight of the big picture. How can you use this situation to your advantage?

Marketing expert and author Jay Abraham believes that strategically oriented companies that are ready to seize an advantage stand to capture 15 percent to 20 percent of the best buyers from their competitors during hard times. By taking a growth-minded strategy, these businesses capture the vast majority of new clients in the market—including those customers that previously didn't have the need for that product or service. So, he explains, if you are positioned to take advantage of adversity, such as a down economy, you can attract all the new buyers in the market. Combine that with the approximately 15 percent to 20 percent of the best, most profitable, most repetitive buyers who used to buy from your competition, and you can double what you might accomplish, even in a strong market.[2]

There are some caveats in being ready to seize the advantage, however. It requires courage, tenacity, and foresight to be ready to endure. It requires an admission when there's trouble, and a proactive impetus to overcome it, not to be a victim of it. In my self-defense training and observance of others, I've seen two kinds of people. And these two categories span both relative novices and those with significant training, quite literally, under their belts. The first type of person doesn't live with an awareness that he will ever really be the victim of an attack or an assault, and will be wholly unprepared if such an incident should ever occur. Caught unawares, this person will make a more compliant victim. The second type is those people who live and train like their life depends on it—because they believe that such an event could occur. They understand that someone, somewhere, could attempt to make them the victim of a violent crime, and they refuse to accept it.

One group internalizes the premise that being attacked is a possibility and, ready to seize victory, won't be defeated. The same is true with small-business leaders. If you understand the threats you face, and are ready for them, you'll be able to manage disadvantage. If you're ready to turn adversity to advantage, you can and will exempt your organization from disaster.

Part of readiness is having taken a position that prevents you from being successfully attacked. The enemy will come, but you can control your readiness:

> The art of war teaches us to rely not on the likelihood of the enemy's not coming, but on our own readiness to receive him; not on the chance of his not attacking, but rather on the fact that we have made our position unassailable.

Sun Tzu tells us that adversity can be a positive force, not just for persevering, but for reigning triumphant. Take to heart this guidance on the strategic value of disadvantage:

> For it is precisely when a force has fallen into harm's way that [it] is capable of striking a blow for victory.

KEEP A POSITIVE FOCUS

If you are able to inspire and maintain a positive outlook throughout your organization, you'll be well on your way to creating the conditions necessary to strike "a blow for victory." A common reaction to adversity is disunity and disharmony, which leads to commiseration and negativity among people. Positivity in leadership is particularly important during these times. Teams can overcome seemingly insurmountable challenges when they are inspired that their fight is worthwhile and success can be achieved:

> When the army is restless and distrustful, trouble is sure to come
> from the other feudal princes. This is simply bringing anarchy into
> the army, and flinging victory away.

Restlessness, distrust, and other forms of negativity must be addressed and overcome. They're a disease that will spread viciously throughout a small business. Instead, strong leaders create a culture of positivity and triumph, even in the face of adversity, and people trust them to lead them to victory.

Marcus Ryu, CEO of Guidewire Software, cofounded the insurance-industry software company in 2001, following the tech crash and 9/11. He acknowledges that it was a counterintuitive time to start a company. As such, a founding principle was to embrace adversity and difficulty. He told the *New York Times* that the people behind Guidewire Software sought to make that a further proof point to their ability to solve difficult problems for clients.[3] Today, Guidewire Software is publicly traded on the NYSE.

Optimism for the future is one of the primary things teams want and need to hear from their leaders, said Ryu. They want honesty, but they also really want hope for the future, a message like: "I stand before you. I'm here for the duration. We've got some challenges. We're equal to them," he said.[4]

The leader who will drive the team to victory despite being, as Sun Tzu says, "in the midst of difficulties," knows that this message has to be delivered, not once or twice, but consistently over and over again.

KNOW WHEN TO FIGHT

Discerning when to fight and when to slip out and save the battle for a more advantageous day with better circumstances is a quintessential principle of Sun Tzu. Sometimes, like on desperate and surrounded ground, fighting is necessary. Other times, it's to your advantage to engage.

On desperate ground, immediate action is required. Remember:

> Ground on which we can only be saved from destruction by fighting without delay, is desperate ground.

As Felix Dennis has concluded of his "victory" over Ziff Davis, and the subsequent carnage (as mentioned in Chapter 2), "My advice on competition is always to ensure that you *want* to fight, and *ought* to fight on a larger competitor's ground. If he is anxious to buy you, determined to park his tanks on your lawn, maybe you should let him. *For the right price.*"[5]

As for smaller players, Dennis advises, "If your competitor is smaller, try to hire him or buy him or join with him. If he won't budge, take drastic action and smash him. If that won't work, then learn to be friends and collude against the woolly mammoths together. But don't fight tigers, my friend. Not if you want to get rich."[6]

Sun Tzu gives us an insightful litmus test for when to engage in battle, and when to abstain. This, too, is a veritable commandment for small-business leaders:

> Move not unless you see an advantage; use not your troops unless there is something to be gained; fight not unless the position is critical.

In that passage above, we see the culmination of perception, understanding, and restraint that the strong general uses to discern when battle is advantageous. Here Sun Tzu provides direction on how to shape a way out of a bad position:

> If we do not want to do battle, even if we merely draw a line on the ground, he will not do battle, because we divert his movements.[7]

DYSON INC.

On a visit to Western Europe, I remember using washrooms in London, Paris, and Italy, and each time being amazed by a powerful, efficient hand dryer. Really, these are the things that make a lasting impression. For years I had wondered why no one has been able to come up with the technology to actually *dry* a patron's hands in a reasonable amount of time. Because of my aversion to touching handles on bathroom doors, I often default to incinerator-fueling hand towels. Imagine my joy upon discovering the Airblade, the invention of Dyson. This fan without external blades dries hands in ten seconds instead of forty, and uses less than a quarter of the energy.[8] After all, speed is important. As Jerry Seinfeld sarcastically said decades ago of using a "hand blower" in the men's room: "I like the hand blower, I have to say. It takes a little bit longer, but I feel when you're in a room with a revolting stench you want to spend as much time as you can."[9]

Most entrepreneurs have compelling stories of beating adversity. But Sir James Dyson's reads like an inventor's grand success story. He finally got a salable vacuum cleaner concept after 5,126 tries and fifteen years of practice. It paid off in a very real sense, as today he's among England's richest people and Dyson makes the bestselling vacuum cleaner, by revenue, in the United States.[10]

But, as with most creators, success wasn't exactly a foregone conclusion. Dyson spent nearly his entire savings to develop his bagless, transparent creation. In addition to debt, frustration, and "soul-destroying drudgery" battling specialists who sought to shoot down his ideas based on their specific expertise, the price of success included lawsuits, too.[11]

Dyson thinks favorably about failure and believes it should be celebrated more, including in schools. Small-business creators need to be able to handle criticism, and they must be endowed with humility, curiosity, determination, and a willingness to try and to fail. After all, he told *Entrepreneur,* "If you want to do something different, you're going to come up against a lot of naysayers."[12] Innovators everywhere are in complete agreement.

Competitors naturally followed the successful Dyson, and other major manufacturers began to market their own cyclonic vacuum cleaners. Dyson sued rivals, including Hoover, for patent infringement. The company won more than $6 million in the Hoover suit. In this way, and through persisting innovation, Dyson has kept the enemy on the move.[13]

PRICELINE

Priceline had all the markings of one of the most tragic dotcom falls from grace. It went online in 1998, when loads of dotcoms, including many of my clients, were running out of all that money that had been growing on trees and scattering throughout the woods, some on fertile soil, some not. You probably remember the earlier and high-visibility days of Priceline's "Name Your Own Price" service for airline tickets. Before ever making a profit in the days of yore, the dotcom had expanded into gas fill-ups, groceries, insurance, mortgages, long-distance phone service, and new car sales.

With these initiatives largely unsuccessful, Priceline lost $1.1 billion in 1999, and in 2000, its stock dipped from $974 to $7 a share.[14]

But the Priceline journey didn't end there. The turnaround started in 2002, when Jeffery Boyd was promoted from general counsel to CEO. He's taken Priceline from a loss of $19 million in 2002 to $1.1 billion in profit in 2011, making it one of Fortune's fastest-growing companies in the United States.[15]

Despite previous downs and further downs, the tremendous asset Priceline had through it all was excellent brand equity, due largely to the company's association with William Shatner in its popular TV commercials. (If you're not sure who Shatner is, you're not old enough to read the sections on Samuel Adams or bourbon.)

To lift Priceline out of the doldrums, Boyd shifted focus back to the travel business, expanding into hotel bookings. While Priceline earned its first ever profit in 2003, the real shift occurred in 2004 and 2005, when the company acquired two hotel reservation sites, in the United Kingdom and Amsterdam, respectively. These buys have been responsible for much of Priceline's growth and stock market success, making them one of the best acquisition stories in Internet history.

The European market for online travel services has substantial room for growth, and Priceline is now venturing into Asia, too.[16]

9

FOCUS

Those of us who've worked for and in small businesses know it all too well. Very often a less structured and even sporadic culture can lead to lack of focus and poor organizational discipline. Its genesis is understandable, entrenched in the breakneck pace and constant change that's required to keep up and to lead the pack. But as we all also know, this situation brings with it some unwelcome by-products that hinder small businesses and force us to play catch-up, duplicate efforts, and otherwise waste time. Sun Tzu called for single-purpose focus for his armies to be successful. Small businesses need this focus, too, if they are going to be market dominators. If that's your goal, you'll do well to implement some of Sun Tzu's instruction on developing and maintaining a focused organization.

Small players have a lot to lose if they don't focus their limited resources on strategic priorities. Whether it's launching a product, starting a new division, or unveiling a marketing campaign, it's important to do it right. Yet far too many ideas fail due to a slow launch, stagnant decision making, or general confusion of purpose. The small business's advantage should be speed to consensus and/or decision making, and rapid mobilization and achievement of goals. It's the unfortunate small business that forsakes that advantage and drains away time tweaking ideas and features in an effort to achieve go-to-market nirvana. Don't get stuck. Build it, release it, and gauge the market's reaction. Always remain focused on the business objectives.

THE LONG GAME

Precision disciplined focus is necessary for big results. It's easy to get distracted from staying the course, but those who do it will have a distinct advantage over all the others in cohesive, long-range results:

> When invading hostile territory, the general principle is, that penetrating deeply brings cohesion; penetrating but a short way means dispersion.

Becoming the dominant player in the long game requires foresight into where the battles will occur and the ability to mobilize forces for victory:

> Knowing the place and the time of the coming battle, we may concentrate from the greatest distances in order to fight.

Of the enemy, Sun Tzu says:

> If he prepares to the front the rear will be weak, and if to the rear, his front will be fragile. If he prepares to the left, his right will be

vulnerable and if to the right, there will be few on his left. And when he prepares everywhere he will be weak everywhere.[1]

The laser-focused small-business leader has fewer vulnerabilities to defend. The better your focus, the fewer your battlefields. And the greater the depth of your focus, the better and more accurately you'll be able to plan even long-range strategies.

ACT ON VICTORIES; CONSOLIDATE RESOURCES

This passage is one of the cardinal principles *The Art of War* holds for small businesses. It's so important because it's so commonly forsaken:

Now, to win battles and capture lands and cities but to fail to consolidate these achievements is ominous and may be described as a waste of resources and time.[2]

Huynh's translation is more clearly and severely worded:

If one gains victory in battle and is successful in attacks, but does not exploit those achievements, it is disastrous.

It's been my experience that this passage gets to the heart of one of the single most costly and detrimental mistakes that small-business practitioners make. Because of shortsighted vision, changes in direction, and limited resources, small businesses too often win victories great and small, but don't fully leverage those opportunities. As a marketing practitioner, I've seen some of these same scenarios get repeated in multiple organizations. Trade shows are a common place for companies of all sizes to lose the plot. These gatherings are considerable spends for organizations, requiring staff resources and carrying hefty costs for the design and production of exhibition booths. Add in sponsorship and other factors, and trade shows can drain an exhibitor's budget by tens of thousands of dollars in one fell swoop. But trade shows are also a tremendous opportunity for interfacing with high-powered partners, existing customers, and future buyers. So what's the problem?

Many times, I see trade show staff aimlessly snatch at "leads" as if they're $100 bills blowing around in a wind tunnel. They grab them and stuff them all together in a lead box or database. But as anyone who is observant and has worked a booth for more than a few minutes knows, not all leads are valuable. Sure, you'll leave the show with a nice haul of so-called leads, but have no sense of which ones are well qualified for immediate follow-up. Real live hot leads can quickly grow cold if prospects are waiting, with credit card in hand, for a salesperson—who delays in calling, because he's sifting through squalor to get to the good opportunities. This is an example of failure to effectively exploit achievements. But it gets worse. Turnover in sales professionals and other mishandling of trade show leads that you've so tirelessly worked to achieve, and at a premium rate, are other sad stories that end up in wasted time, effort, and money.

On the topic of sales professionals, they can be a small business's boon or bane. Some organizations hire, reward, and retain eminently skilled high performers. Others seem to go through sales professionals like they go through socks. Churning through sales professionals is no way to build a business or to consolidate gains. And if this practice describes your organization, there's a very good chance that the problem isn't the salespeople, but your process of selecting, training, retaining, and rewarding them.

I've sat in my share of executive meetings at small businesses, where leaders, who must have had better things to do, quibbled over mundane details that have absolutely no bearing on the bottom line and won't earn the business one solitary dollar. These practices drain the time and energy of smart people. And that's too bad, because small businesses desperately need to leverage the time and energy of all of their people, especially the smartest ones.

Distribution and delivery problems are a devastating way to fail to exploit achievements. (Recall the story of Airwalk in Chapter 5, "Understand the Market.") Focus is required to consolidate hard-fought gains.

EXTEND KNOWLEDGE THROUGHOUT THE ORGANIZATION

Scattering and regrouping was the strategy that Sun Tzu advised General Wu Zixu to deploy to overtake the mighty Chu state. Of this he says:

> Forces achieve missions with unexpectation, take action to fit the advantages, and create diversity through scattering and regrouping.[3]

Large and even midsize organizations are often described as siloed. Business units often work independently, unaware of what's going on in the rest of the organization. But as small-business forces know, siloed doesn't only apply to the bigger guys. Business and technology consulting firms are notoriously siloed. Those who deliver services to government are the guiltiest of all. Consultants often work on long-term contracts in support of a government agency. They're often dedicated on-site with the client and become entrenched in the culture of that agency. They identify their job with that agency as much or more so than they do with the company that employs them. This is outstanding for the relationship with the customer, but it creates a barrier in the sharing of information, innovations, and lessons learned with the rest of the business. This situation creates inefficiencies and pockets of insular knowledge.

In my years of working with government contractors in the Washington, DC, area, I know of one in particular that worked to break that fenced-in model. This intelligence and defense contractor, like many of its peers, prefers the cloak of anonymity. The company makes a concerted and fruitful effort to extend experience and knowledge gained on one project and for one agency throughout other projects and customers. Once a quarter, all employees are assembled and spend the day sharing their best lessons learned, innovations, and methodologies that can be adapted and applied to other customers. Once a year, the company holds a full-scale internal conference for the same purpose.

These sessions take time away from customers. The hours required in the sessions aren't billable hours, and neither is the time spent in travel. But this firm understands that coming together, then distributing even better-informed teams back out to customer sites, makes for stronger employees and happier customers. And, importantly, it makes for a more powerful and dynamic organization in a highly contested and competitive playing field. This is a rare and commendable practice that more consultants and other organizations would do well to emulate.

FOCUS REDUCES MISTAKES

Be firmly fixed on your objectives and the strategies that will lead you to victory, and forsake ancillary activities. This crispness will contribute mightily to strong decision making and reduce mistakes:

What the ancients called a clever fighter is one who not only wins, but excels in winning with ease.

Of his standard for achieving victory, Sun Tzu says:

He wins his battles by making no mistakes. Making no mistakes is what establishes the certainty of victory, for it means conquering an enemy that is already defeated.

DETECT THE ADVERSARY'S DISORDER

Disciplined, wait for disorder; calm, wait for clamor.[4]

By exercising patience and observance, and having enough resources and perspective to wait, perceptive small-business practitioners can detect disorder and clamor among competitors. Or, in the case of Chobani, for example, you can enter a market that's unprepared for you and fill a previously undetected void.

KEEP THE ENEMY ON THE MOVE

This is a concept Sun Tzu visits repeatedly. Stretch your resources while you deplete those of your adversary, and seize the superior position by keeping the competition insecure and on the move. Sun Tzu's direction for smaller forces is something that all small-business leaders should take to heart:

Numerical weakness comes from having to prepare against possible attacks; numerical strength, from compelling our adversary to make these preparations against us.

By encouraging your adversary to always be in preparation for an attack that may come from you, you keep the competition insecure. Legal actions are a public way to do this, and they're often necessary to protect intellectual property. Once James Dyson became successful with his bagless vacuum concept, others began to market their own cyclonic vacuum cleaners; he pursued them for patent infringement and won.[5]

Replete with the necessary infrastructure and resources, large organizations are often quite savvy at keeping the competition on the move. After Samuel Adams went public in 1996, Anheuser-Busch (now Anheuser-Busch InBev) went on the offensive. The beer giant ran ads accusing Samuel Adams of making beer outside Boston and claiming founder Jim Koch was a phony. Koch responded by securing a cease-and-desist ruling from the Better Business Bureau's Advertising Self-Regulatory Council.[6] The better you are able to emulate the standards of Sun Tzu, the more prepared you'll be for anything.

FOCUS ON WHAT'S VIABLE

Ego and shortsightedness can also cause us to fall in love with a concept that has no real market viability. Don't get caught up in drinking your own Kool-Aid. Focus on what will make you money and enable you to achieve your objectives, not on the cool new technology or window dressing.

James Dyson is an inventor and an engineer at heart. In 2001, he brought in Martin McCourt as CEO and launched Dyson in the United States. They developed additional vacuum cleaners and introduced the Contrarotator washing machine. The Contrarotator lost money, and the company pulled the plug on the cool new appliance. Describing his creations as being like his children, Dyson said he didn't like the decision. That's why he had a CEO who was able to make those kinds of tough choices and balance his emotional connection to the products.[7]

> In war, then, let your great object be victory, not lengthy campaigns.

In war and in business, put your energy behind what works and don't waste precious resources on products and services that have no signs of promise.

Sam Adams's Koch isn't afraid to fail. He knows not all beers will be stars. That's why Boston Beer Company discontinues creations that don't gain a foothold. The formula is simple, he told *CNN Money*: "I'm just focused on making great beer and working hard to sell it. If we can get great beer into the mouths of our consumers, we'll do just fine."[8]

WEGMANS

The first time I heard of the Wegmans grocery store chain was when one opened up near the office of an ad agency I worked for near Washington, DC. It seemed like just about every day someone would shop or eat there for the first time and come back raving about it. I joked that it was like a cult. People go in there, have some sort of transformational experience, and they come out converted and a little changed. For weeks I held out because, after all, it's just a grocery store. Who gets excited about grocery shopping? Then, when I finally stopped in during lunch one afternoon, I understood. I've been a convert ever since.

If you live or travel between Massachusetts and Virginia, you are probably familiar with Wegmans. Founded in 1916, the chain has been growing steadily and smartly since it first branched out of New York State. The growth has been calculated. Privately owned, Wegmans answers to its employees and customers. To date, the company maintains locations in six coastal states, despite frequent requests to move outside of its region. In 2011 alone, Wegmans said it received more than 4,400 requests from consumers asking for stores to open in their communities. In that same year, Wegmans marked revenues of $5.6 billion, according to Forbes.com.[9]

But Wegmans won't be lured into territories where it's not prepared to go, nor will it grow more quickly than its plans call for. On its corporate website, Wegmans states it will open only two to three new stores a year. If you happen to have one in your community, you're one of the lucky ones.

––––––

5-HOUR ENERGY

You'll read more later about Manoj Bhargava, founder of Living Essentials, the makers of 5-Hour Energy, because he illustrates some other Sun Tzu attributes. Since he first created his energy shot, Bhargava has known how the product should stand out in the market. He created advertising campaigns that articulated his vision for how best to connect with buyers who had never seen anything like his product. The early 5-Hour Energy TV commercials received very poor industry reviews. But Bhargava is indifferent. He didn't use an ad agency because "they want to win awards; we want to sell stuff," he said in a keynote address. "We wanted to tell people what it does, and they can buy it."[10] That is, after all, the main idea, isn't it?

The commercials didn't win any prestigious awards, but they did increase the product's sales by 50 percent in three months, according to Bhargava. His message was to focus on 5-Hour Energy's value proposition and how it would create an entirely new category.[11]

FIVE GUYS

Five Guys is also mentioned in Chapter 3, "Understand Yourself." That's no coincidence, because a business can't exemplify focus if its leaders don't know who they are and what they do and don't do. From the beginning, Jerry Murrell, the founder of Five Guys restaurants, was adamant that the menu should stay the same: burgers and fries only, and good ones. Quality was paramount. The burgers were handmade, and like everything else in the restaurant, never frozen. Fries were hand-cut and carefully selected from northern U.S. climates.[12]

Now a nationwide chain, Five Guys put a toe in the water to test other menu items. Coffee was a disaster, Murrell said. A chicken sandwich didn't work, either. Today, you can get a hot dog, veggie sandwich, and grilled cheese sandwich at the burger joint. But these additions were considered and implemented carefully. As Murrell told *Forbes,* "My fear was that we'd add something new and not be good at it, then some reviewer would write about how bad our coffee was and not how good our burgers and fries are."[13]

Whereas Wegmans has pursued slow and very calculated growth, Five Guys franchises have been propagating rapidly, with locations in almost every state. According to Murrell, the biggest problem he has with his franchisees is their desire to get him to add more menu items. But Murrell has watched other franchises struggle and he's seen some common themes. He's observed that they've moved away from their core products and tried to do so much, to their detriment.[14]

10

UNITY

U nity is a critical and recurrent theme of Sun Tzu's *Art of War*, but not necessarily one that is highlighted by most authors and Sun Tzu scholars. I am absolutely convinced that this attribute is just as important for small-business practitioners to be able to survive and thrive as it was for Sun Tzu and his military forces. This chapter follows from "Focus" (Chapter 9), because for a team to be unified, its members must understand and share the organization's focus.

This passage speaks volumes about the importance of unity to the small-business leaders who will seek to apply it. Here we see again Sun Tzu's strategy to use the many to attack the few. This is particularly pertinent for small forces:

We can form a single united body, while the enemy must split up into fractions. Hence there will be a whole pitted against separate parts of a whole, which means that we shall be many to the ene-my's few.

As Sun Tzu experienced in his distinguished military career, dividing the enemy is a sound way for a smaller force to see victory. Similarly, it's essential that the small force remains united, even in the face of great adversity.

Joe Calloway has made some observations in his study of extraordinary companies. While these conclusions are important, they certainly aren't revolutionary. It's something we can see and experience in the companies we work for and with and follow in the media. Calloway says that each of these exceptional performers has a clear sense of who they are. They don't define themselves by what they sell. Instead, their sense of "who they are" is measured by their impact on employees, stakeholders, and customers. They're driven to serve, accomplish, and achieve. They also share an ability to differentiate themselves clearly and powerfully.[1]

A small-business leader who can develop this sense of unity would surely revolutionize that entire organization. And a unified organization is one that knows itself well enough to have clear and powerful differentiators. It's a rare and special small business whose entire force has the same goals and objectives and is moving as one unified force. It's much more common to see each player concerned only with her domain and not cognizant of how that work impacts the organization overall. The tolerance for silos in many small businesses is alarmingly and inexplicably high. Instead, small players who want to dominate need to collaborate, learn from each other, and put that learning into action to grow the organization.

Sun Tzu continues his direction on how a small force can divide and defeat a larger one:

And if we are able thus to attack an inferior force with a superior one, our opponents will be in dire straits.

To overtake a larger adversary, be unified and seek to separate the enemy.

SEPARATE THE ENEMY

If his forces are united, separate them.

This passage on reading cues from the enemy doesn't apply only to physical separation, but also to separating morale and causing confusion among the enemy's ranks:

Those who were called skillful leaders of old knew how to drive a wedge between the enemy's front and rear; to prevent co-operation between his large and small divisions; to hinder the good troops from rescuing the bad, the officers from rallying their men.

The consequence, says Sun Tzu, is "to keep them in disorder."

How, then, do you apply Sun Tzu's teachings to unite your forces?

INSPIRE UNITY

Jim Koch was driven by a purpose: "to create a beer revolution in the United States in the same way Samuel Adams created a political revolution," he told *CNN Money*.[2]

Leaders worth following inspire their people not just with clear direction, but with a unified purpose and passionate commitment to a cause:

Hence the experienced soldier, once in motion, is never bewildered; once he has broken camp, he is never at a loss.

When the risk and the odds are greatest, inspired unity is more critical than ever, Sun Tzu says in his direction to an invading force:

The further you penetrate into a country, the greater will be the solidarity of your troops, and thus the defenders will not prevail against you.

The greater the challenge and the mightier the adversary, the stronger the solidarity that will be required of your business.

MAINTAIN THE INSPIRATION

Speed is a tremendous asset in combat, and the advantage of more nimble, flexible small businesses. But as we all know, some campaigns go on longer than we'd like. This is not ideal and can cause stagnation:

When you engage in actual fighting, if victory is long in coming, then men's weapons will grow dull and their ardor will be damped. If you lay siege to a town, you will exhaust your strength.

Inspiring forces to unity is an ongoing initiative, not a once and done proposition. It's critical to ensure that your people hear a clear, consistent, positive message that unites their ranks. If they don't, your organization will be open to risks from without and within:

When the army is restless and distrustful, trouble is sure to come from the other feudal princes.

Sun Tzu's conclusion is clear. If dissention is allowed among the ranks, it will create opportunities for the enemy.

The following passages from the sage may, at first pass, seem difficult to transmit from a military to a business context. But only at first pass:

Throw your soldiers into positions whence there is no escape, and they will prefer death to flight. If they will face death, there is nothing they may not achieve. Officers and men alike will put forth their uttermost strength.

Business is serious, but it's not that serious, at least not to most employees. But, if you are able to instill deep loyalty, you'll build exceptional teams who will serve your customers in exceptional ways. Inspire your people to behave as if it's not just a job, but a cause, and they'll put forth their utmost strength—which, ultimately, will help the entire organization to weather the storms and maintain its talent. The same is true for building an exceptionally loyal customer base.

ZAPPOS

This kind of unity creates a consistent experience for the customer. Zappos CEO Tony Hsieh led the online company from almost no sales to more than $1 billion in gross sales annually. Then he sold the company to Amazon in a deal valued at $1.2 billion. The key to his success has been a culture of customer service and valuing employees. His formula has been to combine profits and passion and give people an opportunity to be part of something bigger than themselves. In his book, *Delivering Happiness,* Hsieh shares some radical concepts, including how Zappos seeks to change the world, and unify customers and employees in that crusade.[3]

Hsieh has said that Zappos decided a long time ago that the brand wasn't going to be limited to the shoes and, later, clothing that the company sold. Instead, Zappos set out to build a brand that was about the very best customer service and customer experience. "We believe that customer service shouldn't be just a department, it should be the entire company," he has said.[4]

According to Hsieh, if they got the culture right, everything else—exceptional customer service, a strong long-term brand, and passionate employees and customers—would occur naturally. To this end, Zappos has turned down many very talented and promising job candidates who could probably very well have brought short-term gains to the bottom line, but who it didn't believe were fits for Zappos culture. The price of that short-term benefit is well worth sacrificing to protect the brand in the long term, he believes.[5] It looks like Amazon agrees.

DISUNITY HAS CONSEQUENCES

These passages speak to Sun Tzu's commitment to the cause, but they also tap into something else. According to Sun Tzu:

> What must unite you is the dire consequences of losing.

Small-business leaders have to be inspiring and uplifting. But should inspiring the forces be done at the risk of omitting the consequences of losing on your business battlefields? Not according to Sun Tzu. Your people must be well acquainted with the consequences of not making their numbers, not hitting deadlines, not delivering, and not accomplishing the mission. They must know what failure will look like to them personally, and to the organization in the aggregate.

RAISE PEOPLE TO GREATNESS

> Gongs and drums, banners and flags, are means whereby the ears and eyes of the host may be focused on one particular point.

In warfare, signals show soldiers when and how to maneuver. Here's the question from the above passage: Is there one particular point on which your people's ears and eyes are focused? Are they poised to act based on those signals? Do they trust the source of the commands and follow accordingly?

If they are united, the bond they build will be felt across the organization:

> When the men are united, the brave cannot advance alone, the cowardly cannot retreat alone. These are the principles for employing a large number of troops.[6]

Even with a small force, you must have a united body that advances together and doesn't retreat. To overtake a larger adversary, unity is even more critical. Inspire your people to greatness, while keeping them cognizant of the steep price of losing. Leave mediocrity for the large organizations, while you demand commitment, loyalty, and performance from everyone on your team.

UNITE WITH THE DEFEATED ENEMY

Remember Sun Tzu's declaration that "the captured soldiers should be kindly treated and kept." Keep this thought in mind in your treatment of former competitors who join your fold, either willingly or less enthusiastically, following a merger or acquisition or the collapse of a competitor.

STAY UNITED ON ALL BATTLEFIELD CONDITIONS

As we saw in the discussion of the various types of ground in "Understand the Market" (Chapter 5), keeping troops moving together is Sun Tzu's explicit direction on many types of ground:

- *On dispersive ground, I would inspire my men with unity of purpose.*
- *On facile ground, I would see that there is close connection between all parts of my army.*
- *On contentious ground, I would hurry up my rear.*
- *On open ground, do not become separated.*[7]
- *On the ground of intersecting highways, I would consolidate my alliances.*
- *On hemmed-in ground, I would block any way of retreat.*

REDUCE DIVISIVENESS

The converse of unity is divisiveness, which can lead to a wave of insubordination that can infect the entire organization. If it's not addressed, it won't go away, but fester, and its ramifications can be disastrous. Sun Tzu says:

When the higher officers are angry and insubordinate, and on meeting the enemy give battle on their own account from a feeling of resentment, before the commander-in-chief can tell whether or not he is in a position to fight, the result is ruin.

WEGMANS

Leadership at the Wegmans supermarket chain understands that loyal and committed employees will foster a spirit of loyalty and commitment among customers. To that end, Wegmans offers college scholarships. Full-time employees can be eligible for four $2,200 scholarships with no restrictions on courses of study. Many employees who receive the scholarship decide to build careers with Wegmans.[8]

According to a company spokesperson, commenting to the *Baltimore Business Journal,* Wegmans has never laid off an employee. Even when sales have slumped and stores have closed, the company has always offered employees jobs in other areas. The Food Marketing Institute reports that staff, who are nonunion, have a turnover rate that's half the industry standard.[9]

Wegmans' high standards may be behind its low turnover rate. In another example of unity, cashiers may not engage with customers until they've completed forty hours of training. The company sends hundreds of staffers across the country, even around the world, to become experts in their products. The company's leaders don't just say employees are important. They show it. When they make decisions, the question is: "Is this the best thing for the employee?"[10]

Their premise is that thinking about employees first will carry through to the customers. A knowledgeable, highly trained, and satisfied employee creates a better experience for customers. This creates loyalty, both in workers and shoppers. The premise is work-ing for the supermarket chain. Across the East Coast, Wegmans stores have the highest average daily sales volumes in the industry.[11]

The Wegmans mission isn't to cure cancer or solve world hun-ger. It's a grocery store. But, like Zappos, it won't be limited by a definition of what the stores sell. The Wegmans brand is also about how the company does business. It encourages employee involve-ment in various community philanthropy programs, which empow-ers them to see their jobs as part of something much larger. In one philanthropic initiative, Wegmans donated 14.9 million pounds of food to community food banks.[12]

"It's really about the community, not the competition," says one Wegmans store manager.[13] But as businesses with the wisdom to be involved in the community know, giving back to the people who support you, in an authentic and meaningful way, is a competitive advantage that creates a unified sense of purpose among everyone it touches.

SALESFORCE.COM

Marc Benioff of Salesforce.com is an essential executive to in-clude in any study of applying Sun Tzu. Protégé of self-proclaimed Sun Tzu student Larry Ellison, Benioff has applied Sun Tzu's tenets throughout his career. He's led Salesforce to change the face of customer relationship management (CRM), and grown it into a global cloud computing company. Benioff told the Sonshi Sun Tzu community that the concept from *The Art of War* that has been most impactful to him is that people can't be united or focused un-less they share a common philosophy that gives their effort a greater meaning. Salesforce believes that companies' missions need to be bigger than making a profit. The company itself gives one percent of its equity, one percent of its profits, and one percent of its employees' time to the community. This helps unite and focus them, and makes for more passionate, valuable employees. Benioff calls it the company's "secret weapon that ensures we always win."[14]

Benioff doesn't seem to see any risk in bringing the weapon out of secrecy and sharing it with the world. He knows, of course, that this is the sort of commitment a competitor can't seek to artificially emulate. It's not like starting a new division, hiring more salespeople, or rebranding the company. No, this is a deep organizational commitment that few are willing to live out.

As with Wegmans, this spirit of unity at Salesforce has been extended to the customer community. Benioff told Sonshi it's an example of *The Art of War*'s "strategic thinking rather than combative thinking." That spirit was foundational in Salesforce's decision to open its platform, which Benioff believes positions the business so that people want to join its mission, instead of attacking it.[15] Nonetheless, there are some great creative combat stories involving Salesforce that you'll read about in the chapter on spirit.

Think about how, on its face, this business decision to open the company's platform sounds antithetical to Sun Tzu. Most leaders would be gripped with terror that their competitors would learn too much or be equipped to discern their moves. But not Salesforce. The company allowed customers to extend their Salesforce applications, and even create and run any type of application on demand. Here's how Benioff characterized the consequence: "By inspiring people to join us and work with us creatively, we gathered an army of innovators who are dedicated to making us better."[16] That's a community of unity, and it's proved to be a powerful force for Salesforce.

It is in Salesforce's competitive tactics, outlined in Chapter 13, "Spirit," where this unity of purpose comes together quite extraordinarily. The company has managed to brilliantly unite a user community with its "end of software" mission. It has been fueled by a purpose to change how the software industry works, by leveraging the lower cost and more robust power of the web, which was a wholly new concept when Salesforce introduced it to the burgeoning CRM world.[17]

PART FOUR

ADVANCED SUN TZU: STRATEGY FOR YOUR SMALL BUSINESS

This part highlights the most difficult and complex aspects of Sun Tzu's grand strategy. These are the elements that are most challenging for readers to understand and apply. This part will explore in detail the absolute primacy of strategy in running a small business, as adapted from Sun Tzu, while maintaining the focus on keeping his more difficult teachings practical for your small business.

This material will challenge you to think differently about how you wage business.

11

MANEUVERING

The seventh chapter of Giles's translation is titled "Maneuvering." Huynh translates this chapter as "armed struggle" and Huang as "armed contention." Our look at the key theme of maneuvering here will be a bit different. We'll focus on adapting *The Art of War*'s teachings on planning movements, shifting position, and changing direction—all fundamental concepts for Sun Tzu. While critical elements of the so-titled chapter are included here, so too are elements of other chapters of *The Art of War* that illustrate how a small business should maneuver to seize and maintain the advantageous position.

Two essential maneuvering concepts discussed previously bear repeating. Keep your competitors moving, and divide them:

If he is taking his ease, give him no rest. If his forces are united, separate them.

Unity, we know, is fundamental to the health of your business. Seek to divide your adversary.

Let's begin with this wonderfully insightful passage from Sun Tzu on tactical maneuvering:

> The best policy in war is to attack the enemy's strategy. The second best way is to disrupt his alliances through diplomatic means. The next best method is to attack his army in the field. The worst policy is to attack walled cities. Attacking cities is the last resort when there is no alternative.[1]

The question you must ask is: What are the most effective ways for you to attack the enemies' strategies? It is my hope that as you study this chapter, you'll remember this question and seek to answer it for your small business.

FIGHTING WITHOUT FIGHTING

As the previous passage indicates in its preference for attacking strategy and disrupting alliances over directly engaging soldiers, the best way to engage in battle is to fight without fighting. Attacking cities is the worst option:

> Therefore the skillful leader subdues the enemy's troops without any fighting; he captures their cities without laying siege to them; he overthrows their kingdom without lengthy operations in the field.

There are many ways for you to capture your competitors' cities without laying siege to them. You can move quietly without gaining the attention of the industry until the appropriate time, buy competitors, hire their top people, absorb or develop exclusive relationships with their best suppliers, and join forces with other smaller forces, as well as other methods. For service businesses with a low volume of customers, you can clandestinely take their best accounts when they are unprepared. You can obtain better suppliers and find better, cheaper ways to get your products to market. You can hire better people and retain them longer than anyone else in your industry. Sun Tzu tells us to never resort to battle unless it's necessary, and never to attack strength for strength.

AVOID STRENGTH AND ATTACK WEAKNESS

This tenet should be the mantra of every small-business practitioner who wants to win. Sun Tzu puts it succinctly:

> In war, the way is to avoid what is strong and to strike at what is weak.

Paychex went where ADP wasn't, and was unwilling to go, instead of fighting this competitor for large and mid-tier payroll accounts. Netflix attacked Blockbuster's inability to adapt. It didn't try to open stores to compete with video rental. Samuel Adams doesn't endeavor to compete with the corporate beer industry monolith Anheuser-Busch InBev or number two, Miller-Coors. Instead, it is competing with other craft beers. These niche players went where the enemy was not and attacked, thereby exploiting the adversary's weakness.

POKE HIM TO SEE WHAT HE'LL DO

> Rouse him, and learn the principle of his activity or inactivity.
> Force him to reveal himself, so as to find out his vulnerable spots.

Test your adversary with feints to gauge his strength and how he'll react. In martial arts or combat sports like boxing and wrestling, the practitioner can lead with some feints to gauge how the opponent will react. By feigning, she can learn that her opponent drops her hands when she counters a punch, or becomes stiff and immobile when she blocks. When you see how your adversary will react to measured attacks, you can maximize future engagements.

TURN DEVIOUS TO DIRECT

Of tactical maneuvering, Sun Tzu says:

> . . . [T]here is nothing more difficult. The difficulty of tactical maneuvering consists in turning the devious into the direct, and misfortune into gain.

As we saw in the chapter on perseverance, and as entrepreneurs know, those who win are able to turn even a potential loss to gain.

Sun Tzu continues:

> Therefore, if you make the enemy's route circuitous and bait him with advantages, though you start out behind him, you will arrive before him.[2]

Sun Tzu directs the general to cause the enemy to take the long way around so that you may get to the destination sooner. Small businesses should be less inclined to reach the same battleground that's being targeted by the bigger businesses. Instead of trying to do something similar to what the powerhouses are doing, build something people will need or want and that they can't get in the way or at the level of quality that you can provide. This is true for really good bourbon, better-quality yogurt, and movies that come to your mailbox or stream to your TV. You may start out after your adversary, but you can get to markets full of new opportunity if you arrive at those niches first.

SEIZE WHAT THE ENEMY CARES ABOUT

> Question: If the enemy is numerous and is advancing in well-ordered arrays, how are they handled?
>
> *Answer: First seize what they care about and they will do as wished.*[3]

This passage requires some examination. How do you capture what your adversary cares about?

Amazon bought all outstanding Zappos shares, options, and warrants for 10 million shares of Amazon's common stock, a value of $807 million. The deal also cost Amazon $40 million in cash and restricted stock that went to Zappos employees.[4]

Ben Parr is the managing partner of the VC fund Dominate-Fund. In addition to recognizing Zappos' growth potential, Parr believes Amazon acquired the company for its extraordinary culture that has led to its dynamic success. Zappos customer service, we have already established, is an essential part of this culture. So too are its leadership and employees, which are also core to why Amazon bought the smaller ecommerce rival. The gigantic Amazon cared about the culture, market share, growth potential, and the core differentiators that caused Zappos to stand out. They paid handsomely for these attributes. This is a valuable lesson in how a smaller business doesn't need to lose its identity or differentiators if it decides to merge or sell. A condition of the deal was that Zappos would still operate in Las Vegas, and the management team would stay intact.[5]

MOVE WITH SPEED

Speed is the essence of war.[6]

Speed is fundamental in business and war. It's even more critical for small businesses, and an easier asset to leverage. With limited resources, small businesses must move with precision in launching attacks and maneuvering. Moving quickly can allow you to achieve a better position than your competitors.

Whoever is first in the field and awaits the coming of the enemy, will be fresh for the fight; whoever is second in the field and has to hasten to battle will arrive exhausted.

Speed, of course, doesn't just apply to how quickly you move against the competition. It also applies to your service and delivery. Agility and responsiveness are among the chief advantages small businesses have over large competitors.

TIMING

Attack him where he is unprepared, appear where you are not expected.

Sun Tzu's direction on taking advantage of opportunity is important, but so too is moving when the market is ready. As we saw in Chapter 2 on applying *The Art of War*, Heaven—which signifies timing—is one of Sun Tzu's five constant factors:

Heaven signifies night and day, cold and heat, times and seasons.

Pascal-Emmanuel Gobry, a *Business Insider Intelligence* analyst, reminds us of the old start-up saying, "Being early is the same as being wrong." Let's use three of his examples for illustrations of the importance of timing in maneuvering.[7]

You may remember using Ask Jeeves. It still exists, now as Ask.com. I loved that search engine, back before Google was part of the vernacular. It was one of the go-to sources for information online, as going to the web for answers began to be the way we found information.

Created in 1998, it was powered by more than 100 editors who monitored human searches, then selected sites that they thought would best answer those queries. The concept was on point, but the technology was not. While Ask Jeeves had pioneered the search engine concept, flaws in the technology and organizational problems, exacerbated by competitors like Google with their natural language search engines, spelled the end of a good run.[8] Ask Jeeves, however, did employ many of the techniques that later made their way into Google, like semantic search and ranking web pages by hyperlinks.[9]

How about SixDegrees.com, the original social network? It was based on the idea that, just as all actors are six degrees or less removed from Kevin Bacon, we're all six degrees away from everyone else on earth. Unfortunately for the company, the world was still flat to a social media innovation.[10]

Then there's LetsBuyIt.com. This pioneering online buying service allowed groups of family and friends to make joint purchases and qualify for big discounts. But this was before social networks were aplenty to propagate offers. Without the intersection of buyers, sellers, and a ubiquitous way to connect them, LetsBuyIt didn't sell. Groupon seems to have learned from this ill-timed failure, as it targets local services from small busi-nesses.[11]

It's not enough for you to be ready. The market has to be ready.

ACHIEVING VICTORY VS. DETERMINING VICTORY

Establishing your strategy is at the heart of small-business ge-nius. It requires formlessness, so it will be a mystery to your com-petition. On being formless, Sun Tzu says:

> How victory may be produced for them out of the enemy's own tactics—that is what the multitude cannot comprehend. All men can see the tactics whereby I conquer, but what none can see is the strategy out of which victory is evolved.

Or, as Huynh translates, with formation, the army achieves victories, yet they do not understand how.

The world may be able to see how you achieve victory. People may see what you are selling and who's buying it. They can see who your partners are and talk to their colleagues about the move-ments you make that can be discerned. But if you are a brilliant strategist, they can't comprehend how you created your victories.

TAKE THE BEST POSITION

The purpose of maneuvering is to be optimally positioned for success:

> The good fighters of old first put themselves beyond the possibil-ity of defeat, and then waited for an opportunity of defeating the enemy.

Total preparation to seize every advantage is a cornerstone of Sun Tzu's direction. Sun Tzu's additional direction here may sound obscure, but let's think about how we can apply it:

All armies prefer high ground to low and sunny places to dark.

How good is your visibility of the landscape that surrounds you? Do you have high ground that comes with good information, trusted sources, and effective communications and intelligence networks? Or do you have low and dark spots that are rife with the unknown? If the latter, you won't be able to put yourself beyond the possibility of defeat and keep your enemy on the move.

Be before the enemy in occupying the raised and sunny spots, and carefully guard your line of supplies.

Guarding your line of supplies speaks to your relationships with suppliers, vendors, and industry partners. By developing alliances and securing investments, you'll keep provisions coming. Shortsighted managers and leaders may treat their vendors poorly, paying them late and even cheating them, and otherwise behaving unprofessionally. The attitude may be that there are plenty of other service providers who will take the business's money. That may be true, but industry and geographic sandboxes are only so big. Eventually, these shortsighted, selfish, scorch-and-burn policies have consequences.

I worked with a firm that made a point of paying print vendors very late and then haggling with them post-delivery on prices that had already been agreed upon. I suppose they thought they won, paying lower rates, and on their terms, but the consequence was that they were blacklisted from the best and most capable printing outfits in town. They were even dropped by a one-of-a-kind shop and unable to find another supplier to meet their requirements. That's no way to do business.

Small-business leaders need all the friends we can get. It's much better business to develop loyal associates and friends, and even develop exclusive relationships, when possible, so the best performers won't provide services or supplies to your competitors. Make enemies of them, and they'll want to help your competitors. They'll even be driven to do so.

BE PROACTIVE

Successful business leaders know that they can't expect to achieve aggressive growth goals if they simply opt to hold ground. None of the companies profiled in these pages achieved any success with a purely defensive long-term strategy:

> If less in number, be capable of defending yourself. And if in all respects unfavorable, be capable of eluding [the enemy]. Hence, a weak force will eventually fall captive to a strong one if it simply holds ground and conducts a desperate defense.[12]

It is in attacking that you'll be strong, not in defending:

> Standing on the defensive indicates insufficient strength; attacking, a superabundance of strength.

THE ARMY ON THE MARCH

If your army is on the move, Sun Tzu says:

We come now to the question of encamping the army, and observing signs of the enemy. Pass quickly over mountains, and keep in the neighborhood of valleys.

Do not be observed by the enemy as you make your plans and carry them out. Keeping your intentions hidden is especially difficult now that so much is in the public domain, so you must work to mask your secret movements more than ever. While keeping an eye to strategy and hiding your movements, consider the path of least resistance so that you may move quickly over difficult terrain.

After crossing a river, you should get far away from it.

The Art of War application here is that once you've succeeded in a maneuver, don't allow your business to get pushed back into a less favorable position. It's not enough to achieve a victory. You must be able to sustain it. Not long ago I met with a small business that's poised to exploit a void in the market. The company's leaders have an innovative solution for niche medical practices. One of the ways they validated opportunity was by watching a competitor that made significant inroads by selling into the base. But that competitor soon burned through so many resources to acquire these contracts that it was unable to deliver and had to close the business.

If you don't have a strategy and resources to continue to maneuver amid obstacles, this tragic story could be yours as well.

In crossing salt-marshes, your sole concern should be to get over them quickly, without any delay.

Don't linger on unwelcome ground. When in a compromised position, make your decisions quickly and don't waver. Many executives cite one of their greatest regrets as clutching on to underperformers for longer than was sensible. David Astorino, a senior partner at RHR International, said that when many CEOs reflect on what they'd do differently in their careers, "they almost always say, 'I knew in my gut that was not going to work with that individual, and I wish I had trusted that gut feeling and made that decision faster.'"[13] This kind of well-intended procrastination can cause real damage to a small business, and spark delays and stagnation throughout the organization.

NETFLIX

The Netflix story began in 1997 when founder Reed Hastings got a $40 late fee from a video store for an *Apollo 13* VHS rental. Then and there, he started thinking about the viability of a movie-rental-by-mail concept. He began by mailing DVDs to himself. When they arrived in pristine condition, he believed he was onto something. He described to *CNN Money* the enchanting moment when he knew it was going to work:

> "I was down in Arizona in 2003, visiting one of our distribution centers on the outskirts of Phoenix. It was raining, and my umbrella wasn't working, so I walked the half mile from the distribution center to the hotel. I got the message on my BlackBerry that we hit a million [subscribers] that day while I was walking in the rain. It was this beautiful moment where I was just so elated that we were going to make it, and that was also the first quarter that we turned profitable. It was a magic walk."[14]

Netflix has been well positioned to succeed. Consumers have an insatiable hunger for entertainment, and they are increasingly leveraging streaming. Hastings and the leadership at Netflix have demonstrated their skill in staying on the cusp of the market's demands, even with iconoclast moves that have been criticized. Their decision to promote streaming at the expense of their DVD business prompted considerable skepticism. In 2011, Hastings split Netflix into two businesses, DVD and streaming, and allowed them to compete with each other for customers. Most consumers wouldn't want to pay for both, so they had to pick one.[15]

To the critics' surprise, Netflix grew revenue and profits while encouraging customers to make the transition from DVDs to streaming. But in retrospect, we can see why this decision worked. They refused to sacrifice weakness for strength and cling to a model that was coming outmoded. Hastings was able to pull cash out of the DVD side of the house to pay for building the faster-growing but lower-margin streaming business. Netflix succeeded in growing revenue and profits, while making the market transition from the DVD platform to streaming.[16] This is a brilliant move that illustrates how to *carefully guard your line of supplies.* The on-demand streaming market is heating up with competition, but Netflix remains well positioned.

Adam Hartung concluded in *Forbes* the rarity of this victory: "Almost no company pulls off this kind of transition," he wrote. Instead, most fight tooth and nail to defend a losing territory for too long, and miss opportunities to evolve. It was a much smarter move to capture the burgeoning market for streaming, instead of clinging to a waning business. Perhaps Netflix learned from Blockbuster.[17]

It's also possible that they learned from Sun Tzu in the passage earlier in this chapter:

> A weak force will eventually fall captive to a strong one if it simply holds ground and conducts a desperate defense.[18]

12

ADAPTATION

Connected tightly with maneuvering and overall strategy, innovation is part of the culture of many small businesses. It's the not-so-secret sauce that has forged the path to industry hegemony for the players who maintain that intrepid edge. Small businesses have an advantage in being better able to apply tactics to a dynamic, fluid reality than their larger competitors. But to remain viable, they must continue to innovate.

Small-business practitioners are all too familiar with the grim statistics that 80 percent of new businesses fail within the first five years. But what's even more interesting is that many of the 20 percent that succeed take a different path than the one they started down—in some cases much different. We'll turn now to Sun Tzu's direction on thriving by changing strategies and tactics.

VARY PLANS

Sun Tzu's successful general must be adept at varying plans. Even though he's well versed in the five constant factors as described in Chapter 2—Moral Law (i.e., "The Way"), Heaven, Earth, the Commander, and Method/Discipline—that won't be enough:

> The student of war who is unversed in the art of war of varying his plans, even though he be acquainted with the Five Advantages, will fail to make the best use of his men.

The ability to vary tactics is critical for Sun Tzu. The leader who is skilled in this regard is capable, but the one who isn't will be unable to gain traction:

> The general who thoroughly understands the advantages that accompany variation of tactics knows how to handle his troops. The general who does not understand these, may be well acquainted with the configuration of the country, yet he will not be able to turn his knowledge to practical account.

Flexibility in accordance with real and dynamic circumstances is essential in war, as is it in business:

> Be flexible and decide your line of action according to the situation on the enemy side.[1]

THE WATER METAPHOR

Sun Tzu, like many Asian and Asian-inspired philosophers, including martial artist Bruce Lee, uses water to model how we should engage with an adversary. Water flows around or over a force. It adapts and changes shape. It encompasses an infinite variety of plans, to avoid what is strong and to strike at what is weak. You've seen this concept illustrated repeatedly in these pages. Rather than rigidly committing to staying a course, the businesses that have overcome the odds have illustrated Sun Tzu's meditations on water. Their tactics have modeled water in their adaptability, fluidity, and shapelessness. Below we have a few passages from Sun Tzu on water as a metaphor for battle:

> Military tactics are like unto water; for water in its natural course runs away from high places and hastens downwards.
>
> Water shapes its course according to the nature of the ground over which it flows; the soldier works out his victory in relation to the foe whom he is facing.
>
> Therefore, just as water retains no constant shape, so in warfare there are no constant conditions.

Sun Tzu makes that passage even more applicable with this next sentence:

> He who can modify his tactics in relation to his opponent and thereby succeed in winning, may be called a heaven-born captain.

Online photo-sharing, video-sharing, and social networking service Instagram began as the location-based social network Burbn. Uploading and sharing photos was just one feature of Burbn, but it's the one that took off with users and shaped Instagram into the service it is today.[2] There are many other, similar success stories of businesses that plotted a very different course than the one they initially conceived. The commonality among them all is the ability to adapt and respond to opportunity.

Identify and follow the trends in your industry. Don't fight against the current of change. Instead, recognize these as an opportunity and seize the advantage. Tablet and smartphone sales were exploding, as sales of DVD players were leveling. Netflix has capitalized on this trend and sought to capture a burgeoning market, rather than one with waning demand.

INFINITE VARIETY

Sun Tzu says that to always stay ahead of the enemy, you must continually devise new tactics, not return to those previously used, even if used successfully:

> Do not repeat the tactics which have gained you one victory, but let your methods be regulated by the infinite variety of circumstances.

This is one more reason not to openly engage in battle any more than is necessary. You won't have to keep coming up with new methods and unexpected methods of attack. To be innovative is to hide your objectives from your competitors:

> He shifts his campsites and undertakes marches by devious routes so as to make it impossible for others to anticipate his objective.[3]

By making continuous improvements in your business, you are contributing to Sun Tzu's call to develop an infinite variety of tactics. Business author John Spence has said that the competitive advantages of old were access to capital, proprietary technology, location, one-of-a-kind distribution channels, and economies of scale. These are less essential today. Instead, the winners of the future, he says, will forge new competitive advantages based on ongoing and incremental improvements to every single aspect of their business.[4] How are you continually making ongoing and incremental, or even very large, improvements in every aspect of your business?

BE DISRUPTIVE

If you're like me, you heard the word *disruptive* a lot as a kid. But when it comes to innovation, disruption can be a very good thing. In 1997, Harvard Business School professor Clayton Christensen detailed an interesting premise in his book, *The Innovator's Dilemma*. He said that as companies innovate at a more rapid pace than their customers' needs demand, most organizations eventually develop products or services that are overkill for most customers in their market. They're too sophisticated, expensive, or complicated for the majority of buyers. Nonetheless, businesses pursue the higher-priced products and services suitable for their most lucrative customers. It's with these buyers at the higher tier of the market where they'll make most of their money. This dynamic, he says, creates an opportunity for "disruptive innovation," to serve less profitable customers at the bottom of the market.[5]

Examples of this disruption include the changeover from mainframe computers to minicomputers, film to digital, four-year colleges to community colleges, traditional doctor's offices to retail medical clinics, to name a few. With disruptive innovation, smaller businesses bring solutions to market to capitalize on the opportunities posed by lower-margin products and solutions. In so doing, they can revolutionize industries.[6]

This is an extremely important dynamic for innovative small businesses to understand. In the years since *The Innovator's Dilemma* was published, this trend has accelerated. As Steve

Denning wrote in *Forbes*, the life expectancy of Fortune 500 firms has dropped to less than fifteen years.[7]

Christensen uses the example of router technology. Cisco Systems was a disruptor, offering an alternative to the circuit switching equipment made by Lucent and Nortel. Router technology was cheaper, but not good enough for voice data transfer. And as customers were unfamiliar with the potential of this technology, there was absolutely no customer demand for it. However, with continuous improvement to its router technology, Cisco succeeded in making it fast enough for voice. While Cisco is a case study of a business capable of adapting to change during its years in business, it is now threatened by innovators of blade servers and soft switches.[8]

Salesforce is one of those smart larger organizations. Like Apple and Amazon, it is cited by Christensen as employing a model focused on more than short-term profitability, but also on continuous innovation and experimentation. These companies also share very high marks for satisfaction from their customers. This model drives companies to consistently innovate and to disrupt—even within their own businesses.[9]

STEALTH

If you set a fully equipped army in march in order to snatch an advantage, the chances are that you will be too late. On the other hand, to detach a flying column for the purpose involves the sacrifice of its baggage and stores.

If a large army or a large division advances entirely, it must do so more slowly than its smaller, stealthier counterparts. By sending in a smaller force, the large army has only a portion of its strength and resources, lacking the full bore of armaments and provisions to attack and defend. This is another reason why keeping the enemy on the move is important, especially for smaller players.

> Thus, if you order your men to roll up their buff-coats [which Huynh translates as armor], and make forced marches without halting day or night, covering double the usual distance at a stretch, doing a hundred LI in order to wrest an advantage, the leaders of all your three divisions will fall into the hands of the enemy.

He goes on to warn that a forced march will mean that significant portions of the army won't reach its destination, division leaders will be lost, and provisions and supplies will be sacrificed. It's far more burdensome and logistically intensive to keep a large entity supplied and functioning than it is to move a smaller, more nimble counterpart. You should always seek to leverage your advantage of stealth for your business.

PAYPAL

It took several years of trial and error and overcoming serious problems with user fraud for PayPal to become the default online payment system for millions of users. The initial start-up concept in 1998 was a business called Fieldlink, which developed cryptography for handheld devices. After building a platform that never caught on, founders Max Levchin and Peter Thiel changed the business name to Confinity and moved into sending IOUs from one PalmPilot user to another. With no traction gained there, and success contingent on the ubiquity and health of the PalmPilot market, they shifted course again, this time to a payment system called Pay-Pal. This concept moved them to e-mail payments via the web. All of these very rapid changes occurred within the course of about fifteen months, according to Reid Hoffman, former PayPal executive vice president.[10]

Much of PayPal's early growth as a payment system can be attributed to eBay users. This community promoted the platform to others as an easy, safe, and trustworthy way to exchange money. While eBay had an internal payment business, Billpoint, users preferred PayPal. Hoffman asked the team, "What's this eBay thing and why are people using it?" The answer followed quickly: "Oh my gosh, there are our customers," Hoffman remembered thinking. Those users proved to be a very fruitful market for PayPal.[11] In 2002, PayPal went public and was bought by eBay for $1.5 billion. The entire story unfolded in less than four years. Not bad for a few drastic course corrections.

PRICELINE

Priceline.com is covered in Chapter 8, "Perseverance." But theirs is also a story of adaptation, and the value of folding in powerful alliances. Jay Walker was the brain behind the "Name Your Own Price" system, which he developed and applied to the airline industry. By 1997, his company, Walker Digital, implemented the concept for Priceline.com's ticketing service. The airlines resisted this bold new model. After all, the industry didn't invent it, so how good could it be? That was the old-timey, traditional thinking, anyway. Walker was successful in attracting two relatively small airlines, TWA and America West.[12]

The popular advertising campaign featuring William Shatner would follow. Pre-revenue, the company paid Shatner in part with shares in Priceline.com. The ads were a success. But driving people to the website, it turned out, wasn't a panacea. Priceline sold more than 30,000 tickets in its first two months, but it couldn't meet the demand through TWA and America West alone. To make up for this shortfall, it had to buy tickets for other airlines on the retail market and subsidize customer orders. The company lost money.[13]

By bringing in the former president of Citicorp, Richard Braddock, as CEO, the company bolstered its legitimacy. Priceline was then able to sign its first major airline, Delta, in a deal that included giving 12 percent of its stock to Delta. Other airlines followed this big dog.[14]

Priceline went public on the NASDAQ in 1999, and became a cool tech-boom rock star. Following that, hard times came from various sources: overreach into disparate markets, the bursting of the dotcom bubble, trauma in the airline industry, and the opening up of ticket sales via the Internet.[15] You'll find more about how the story is playing out in "Perseverance," including how Priceline has adapted its model to accommodate changes in the market.

PayPal and Priceline represent two very different examples of adaption. The Priceline story is one of fitting the concept to a huge and changing market, and readapting when it wasn't successful. The PayPal story is of quickly adapting the core of the business, and then doing so again . . . and again . . . until a valid idea takes root. In both cases, these adaptations are much more than footnotes for the archives. They opened up new revenue opportunities, blazed new trails, and harnessed disruption. Company leaders demonstrated the foresight to see that the course they were on needed to be modified, or shifted entirely, and they were willing to do it.

Are you?

13

SPIRIT

It's usually called something like "attitude." Motivational business literature and life coachery are replete with it. The law of attraction tells us that like attracts like. The more positive and upbeat we are, the more likely we are to attract other positive and encouraging people. But for Sun Tzu, this quality is a uniquely powerful force capable of shaping military hegemony. *The Art of War* can't really be understood without a study of the somewhat abstract element of spirit.

THE SPIRIT OF WIND, FOREST, FIRE, MOUNTAIN, NIGHT, AND THUNDERBOLT

This passage combines elements of classical writings from before Sun Tzu's time:[1]

Let your rapidity be that of the wind, your compactness that of the forest. In raiding and plundering be like fire, in immovability like a mountain. Let your plans be dark and impenetrable as night, and when you move, fall like a thunderbolt.

Let's explore these attributes and what they mean for your small business:

Rapid like the wind. Wind is formless. It feels like it comes from nowhere. It can't be grasped, and it easily shifts and changes direction. It can be extraordinarily powerful. Sun Tzu calls for movement like the wind, not only in speed, but in adaptability and coordinated force. The application for your small business it that your maneuvers should be unable to be predicted. They should happen quickly, and they should be powerful enough to achieve the intended results.

Compactness like the forest. Compactness, when coupled with rapidity, speaks to movement that is tight and coordinated. In fact, other translations prefer *march like the forest*. If your people are unified and move together, they will be much more difficult to divide. Forests are also thick and dense. The competition can't see through to the end or exploit weak openings, so it may be overwhelmed by the appearance of force. Your small business's movement should have every appearance of coordination and unification, unless you are trying to lure him in by feigning disorder.

Raid and plunder like fire. Fire burns and destroys rapidly and completely, as it creates fear and chaos. When you execute a clear strike, you should do so with unabashed power and commitment. Speed is again essential.

Immovability like a mountain. Despite how well his course is planned, the extraordinary leader is able to modify his tactics in relation to shifting circumstances. You must adapt to changing conditions, but be as determined for victory as an immovable mountain. The unity of your team is a critical factor here. Division within your ranks will have the opposite effect, undermining your determination and making you more vulnerable to the strikes of your competition.

Plans as dark and impenetrable as night. Your next steps should be a mystery to the competition, and your business should have safeguards in place to ensure that this is the case.

Fall like a thunderbolt. In his translation Huang refers to the darkness *as unpredictable as rain clouds, striking like thunder and lightning.* Lightning will go through anything to reach the ground. Like fire, thunder and lightning can cause chaos, and lightning can be fatal. Like the wind, it appears to come from nowhere. At close range, thunder can be deafening, which only adds to the clamor and confusion. All of these phenomena speak to the criticality of making your attacks definitive, well coordinated, and impeccably timed.

These elements illustrate the importance of creating chaos and uncertainty among the competition, bringing full power and concerted energy to bear, and leveraging intense speed. They are all important attributes for effective martial artists, too.

Speed, economical movements, and veiled intentions allow strikes and throws to have exponentially greater impact. It's the idea of falling like a thunderbolt that resonates most deeply for me. In jujitsu, we train to be ready for any conceivable attack. Rather than allowing the mind to be distracted by trying to guess what attack will come during the heat of combat, the idea is this: It doesn't matter what comes. I'm ready for it. That doesn't just mean being ready to defend against a ferocious attack, but preparedness to turn that attack on its head and discourage, damage, or destroy an adversary. Like thunder, a defense can be coupled with a deafening and powerful yell that comes from the center that we call a *kiai*. And like lightning, we stop at nothing short of going through enemies who aim to harm us.

WIN FIRST

This is one of the single most important concepts from all of Sun Tzu. It's meaningful both for business leaders and for individuals on their career path:

> In war the victorious strategist only seeks battle after the victory has been won, whereas he who is destined to defeat first fights and afterwards looks for victory.

The idea here is that if we are to be triumphant, the victory must occur *before* the battle. This directive applies to preparation, as well as to all of Sun Tzu's directions to be well trained and well positioned for victory. But it's greater than that. If you've done all the proper planning and preparation, yet you don't believe you will win, your chances are profoundly diminished. As Henry Ford famously said, "Whether you think you can, or you think you can't—you're right." Sun Tzu would say Ford was right.

Martial arts contain this irony. I've trained with many people in a variety of different schools. The purpose of martial arts, for me at least, is self-defense. The most important consideration in all of self-defense training is this: Can you defend yourself in the face of violent adversaries? It comes down to the decision you've already made either to be a victim or not to be a victim. Rank and experience are less important than the spirit and "win first" mind-set of the individual. I've seen black belts who I don't think could defend themselves against a moderately skilled adversary their own size, let alone multiple armed attackers. I remember a woman who had been training for several years telling me, "I don't think I could ever hit a man and hurt him."

"Never hit a man and hurt him . . ." If I believed that, I'd never leave my house.

Sun Tzu's idea here is that victory proceeds battle, both in practical terms and in the spirit that says, "I won't be a victim," or "I'm going to get this promotion," or "This account is mine." Much more than wishful thinking, if you adopt and apply it, the character of winning before fighting will forever change how you do business.

KEEP THEM SHARP

Sun Tzu is adamant that victories should be achieved as quickly as possible. One of the most important by-products of that is the morale of the people fighting for him:

> Again, if the campaign is protracted, the resources of the State will not be equal to the strain.

One of the greatest resources he had—and that you have—are people.

> Now, when your weapons are dulled, your ardor damped, your strength exhausted and your treasure spent, other chieftains will spring up to take advantage of your extremity. Then no man,

however wise, will be able to avert the consequences that must ensue.

When you are depleted, you're weak and vulnerable. Look for these same indicators in your competitors and time your movements against them. These are opportunities to turn their disadvantage to your advantage.

Small-business leaders should always remember Sun Tzu's call to be good stewards of the people who trust you, to honor their strength and skill and give them the resources they need to win. Sharp people won't work for very long for dull organizations that don't endeavor to bring out their best.

They won't tolerate organizations that can't accomplish objectives and seize opportunities, either. As Sun Tzu says:

> Thus, though we have heard of stupid haste in war, cleverness has never been seen associated with long delays.
>
> Therefore, in the beginning morale is high, then slackens, and at last dissipates.[2]

You must keep morale high, not only in the beginning, when it's easiest, but continually between and throughout engagements.

TAKE ADVANTAGE OF THE OPPOSITION'S LOW SPIRIT

Study your adversary so that you can use the ebbs and flows of the strength of his spirit:

> A clever general, therefore, avoids an army when its spirit is keen, but attacks it when it is sluggish and inclined to return. This is the art of studying moods.

How will you take advantage of it?

DESTROY THEIR ALLIES' MORALE

Not only should you look to damage the spirit and unity of the adversary, but also look to harm that of their allies and support networks:

> When a warlike prince attacks a powerful state, his generalship shows itself in preventing the concentration of the enemy's forces. He overawes his opponents, and their allies are prevented from joining against him.

You can look to develop exclusive and/or more fruitful relationships with your competitors' allies, or position yourself with key trusted sources to gain intelligence on your competition. How else can you disrupt your competition's alliances?

EXPLOIT THE OPENING

Preparation and timing are critical in creating and taking advantage of gaps in the enemy's ability to launch attacks or provide defenses. But the role of spirit that acts decisively is unrivaled:

> At first, then, exhibit the coyness of a maiden, until the enemy gives you an opening; afterwards emulate the rapidity of a running hare, and it will be too late for the enemy to oppose you.

Now only *can* you exploit openings, but for Sun Tzu it's a mandate:

> If the enemy leaves a door open, you must rush in.

CONQUER AN ENEMY ALREADY DEFEATED

> He wins his battles by making no mistakes. Making no mistakes is what establishes the certainty of victory, for it means conquering an enemy that is already defeated.

What does it mean to conquer an enemy already defeated? Flawless execution is clearly part of this directive. But Sun Tzu goes on:

> Hence the skillful fighter puts himself into a position which makes defeat impossible, and does not miss the moment for defeating the enemy.

Sun Tzu calls for vigilance to seize every opportunity to defeat the enemy. The strong leader knows when she has the superior position, understands the condition of the adversary's relative strength or weakness, and has the wherewithal to rapidly and decisively attack and win.

Huynh translates this passage as follows:

> No miscalculations means the victories are certain, achieving victory over those who have already lost.

Follow Sun Tzu's direction and take on the battles wherein there are the fewest opportunities for miscalculations.

BE IRRESISTIBLE

This is another mandate for a strong spirit that the small-business leader should heed:

Therefore the good fighter will be terrible in his onset, and prompt in his decision.

Huang translates the passage this way:

Those sophisticated in battle have combat power that is irresistible and a restrained release of force that is instantaneous.

Consider the importance of prompt and committed decision making in your organization's ability to deliver a "restrained release of force."

Sun Tzu continues his discussion of dispensation of energy:

Energy may be likened to the bending of a crossbow; decision, to the releasing of a trigger.

Timing and decisiveness are key points. The question for the entrepreneur and small-business executive is, How are you setting the crossbow? Do you know when to release the trigger?

Not all business leaders are good, reliable decision makers. Many times younger, less experienced, and uncertain managers have tendencies to second-guess their decisions and shift directions. This causes the workforce to stall. Eventually, they'll be conditioned to operate at a sluggish pace because it's in their best interests. Why should they move quickly to put a plan into action if they believe their leadership will shift course the next day? That's failure to consolidate wins, and it's at best foolish and at worst disastrous for small businesses.

In addition to causing slow movement, thereby dulling a key small-business advantage, this muddy decision making also mutes enthusiasm and causes confusion in the ranks. If you've made it this far into *The Art of War for Small Business,* you know that these are all very dangerous by-products that will threaten the small business that suffers from them.

WHAT ATTACKING WITH FIRE TELLS US ABOUT SPIRIT

Chapter 12 of *The Art of War* is a short chapter on use of fire in attacks. Elements of this chapter are an illustration of spirit.

> In order to carry out an attack, we must have means available. The material for raising fire should always be kept in readiness.

We should also be physically prepared and of substantial spirit to launch an attack. Sun Tzu writes of preparation to meet five possible developments, including fire:

> When fire breaks out inside to enemy's camp, respond at once with an attack from without.

Be prepared to swoop in when there is confusion, disruption, and disorder. This is true whether you attack, as Sun Tzu directs here, or if you seize an opportunity caused by other conditions, including the enemy's misfortune.

Or as Chicago Mayor Rahm Emanuel has said, "You never want a serious crisis to go to waste."

SALESFORCE'S SPIRIT

*T*he *Art of War* gave Marc Benioff, CEO of Salesforce.com, the confidence he needed to enter an industry dominated by much bigger players. "Ultimately, it's how [we] took on the entire software industry," Benioff wrote in the foreword to *The Art of War: Spirituality for Conflict.*[3] Benioff is a tech industry rock star—and an enthusiastic student of Sun Tzu. In Benioff's example you'll find some very rich illustrations of Sun Tzu's tactics, as executed by a professional who's well versed in the sage's teaching. Benioff also has quite a sense of humor. (Kudos to Julie Bort of *Business Insider,* for providing a nice summary of the top scenes from the highlight reel.)

A famous incident occurred shortly after Salesforce.com's launch. In a very clever move, the company hired actors as "protesters," along with a fake TV crew, at a Siebel Systems user conference. A huge player, Siebel (now part of Oracle Corporation) was Benioff's biggest rival. Salesforce was introducing a bold new way to deliver customer relationship management (CRM) software via the web. The "protesters" picketed the venue with signs chanting, "The Internet is really neat . . . Software is obsolete!" and "NO SOFTWARE."[4]

That incident was so high profile, it encouraged Siebel to protest in its own way and call the police. Benioff said the play aroused the adversary's emotions, which he recognizes as a page out of the sage's *Art of War* playbook.[5]

But I think this next example from the Benioff chronicles is my favorite.

At yet another Siebel event, this one in Cannes, France, Benioff and company rented all the airport taxies that went from Nice to Cannes—"capturing" most of the attendees—then used the forty-five-minute drive to pitch Salesforce. Again, Siebel called the police.[6]

Microsoft was paying attention to Benioff's attention-generating, over-the-top, hit-and-run ways to get to the competition. In 2010, Microsoft hired people to ride Segways at a Salesforce conference and carry an ad featuring a man, presumably a corporate user, that said, "I didn't get forced." As in "salesforced." If Microsoft's play on words was clever, Benioff's response was incomparable. During his keynote speech he brought to the stage the man who had been featured in the ad and begged the fake customer to use Salesforce. The actor agreed, and the crowd stood and cheered.[7]

In another high-profile exhibition, Benioff was slated as the keynote speaker at Oracle's OpenWorld conference in 2012. Larry Ellison, Oracle cofounder and CEO, is Benioff's mentor and former boss. He's also a student of Sun Tzu, and the firms are rivals. That combination makes for a very interesting playing field. When Oracle announced it would move Benioff's speech to later in the week, he protested, saying, "The show is over." Benioff issued a press release and tweeted that Oracle had "canceled his keynote" and that he would deliver it at a nearby hotel restaurant.[8]

The Salesforce CEO used the venue change to showcase the Chatter product, in a turn of events that just might have meant he reached a much bigger live audience. He drew characteristic attention by postulating that his company's cloud, nonproprietary software is "contrarian," and that his speech was rescheduled because of the threat Salesforce poses to Oracle. Benioff took it even further and used the situation to illustrate how quickly and effectively his people could move to get the new venue, posters, and promotion, all using Salesforce's Chatter social network. Benioff said it was something he doubted the company could have pulled off a few years earlier,[9] although they probably could have done *something* to get attention.

Of his tactics to raise the ire of Siebel, Benioff said they illustrated two of Sun Tzu's directives:

* *Appear at places where he must rush to defend, and rush to places where he least expects.*
* *Those skilled in warfare move the enemy, and are not moved by the enemy.*[10]

14

DECEPTION

S mall businesses can leverage deception to confuse and disrupt their competitors. You can even allow the misperceptions of competitors to work against them and in your favor. You know that the current business cosmos offers unprecedented opportunity for forward-thinking start-ups and virtual businesses to create and shape a perception that allows them to survive and thrive among big business adversaries. Should small businesses puff up how they are perceived in order to look bigger than they are? Or should they fly under the radar until it's time to leverage a well-timed assault? Or can the answer for your business be a combination of both?

My focus in this chapter is on ethical ways of leveraging deception, misinformation, and intelligence to wage business. I'm not suggesting dishonestly because it's not how I do business. War, on the other hand, is a different matter.

All warfare is based on deception.

Deception is a keystone of *The Art of War*. But what does this quintessential, oft-cited passage from Sun Tzu mean for small-business leaders today?

CONTROL AND SHAPE APPEARANCES

Sun Tzu instructs that the superior general will shape how his forces are perceived by the adversary, and that he will keep his plans hidden. In "Spirit" (Chapter 13), we studied his direction on how to be like wind, forest, fire, mountains, dark, and thunder in your actions. Remember this mandate:

> Let your plans be dark and impenetrable as night, and when you move, fall like a thunderbolt.

Beyond keeping our plans out of the reach of adversaries, Sun Tzu calls for controlling how the enemy perceives us:

> When able to attack, we must seem unable; when using our forces, we must seem inactive; when we are near, we must make the enemy believe we are far away; when far away, we must make him believe we are near.

The example I use in *Sun Tzu for Women* to illustrate this principle of appearing to be something we're not is still my favorite. Marsha Serlin started United Scrap Metal Inc., in 1978, with only $200 and a rented truck. She was repeatedly underestimated in those early years, the lone woman in a boys-only club. After the novelty wore off as far as the competition was concerned, she flew under the radar, Sun Tzu style. Her operations were run out of a ramshackle old building she said was reminiscent of the *San-ford and Son* set. The façade was intentional. As the business grew, Serlin clandestinely purchased all the property behind it. She successfully turned the devious to the direct. Today, United Scrap processes 140,000 tons of steel a year and achieved $250 million in revenue in 2012.

Another excellent example of a business shaping perception is Carnival Cruise Lines, the largest cruise line in the world. Yes, the brand has had some very public disasters, and we'll see how smooth the sailing is for the company in the near and long term. But Carnival's early days provide some useful illustrations of shaping perception, as well as forging mighty alliances, as mentioned in Chapter 6. When the cruise line started, it had one ship and no real capital. Because it could only afford to paint one side of the ship, Carnival docked it with the painted side facing out.[1]

USING AND CREATING CHAOS

Sun Tzu is a proponent of creating the outward appearance of chaos and confusion to lure in the adversary. This strategy brings with it certain risks to businesses operating in an open and transparent world. You don't want any appearance of weakness or confusion to influence your customers, partners, or potential investors.

The story of United Scrap Metal's early days once again illustrates what Sun Tzu says about the appearance of chaos:

> Amid the turmoil and tumult of battle, there may be seeming disorder and yet no real disorder at all; amid confusion and chaos, your array may be without head or tail, yet it will be proof against defeat.

But creating such an appearance of disorder and weakness requires strength and discipline:

> Simulated disorder postulates perfect discipline, simulated fear postulates courage; simulated weakness postulates strength.

Sun Tzu is saying that only the structured, strategic, and strong leader can successfully demonstrate the appearance of chaos and weakness to the adversary—and use it to his advantage. This is a much more nuanced consideration for your small business, however. Appearances of weakness, disorder, and fear should never be allowed to damage the public perception of your business, unless it is for a very short period of time and with the victory close at hand. The balance of power must quickly shift back in your favor. No matter how well or how poorly you are doing, what matters most is how well your customers and market influencers think you're doing. Employees, of course, matter too.

LURE THE ENEMY

> Thus one who is skillful at keeping the enemy on the move maintains deceitful appearances, according to which the enemy will act. He sacrifices something, that the enemy may snatch at it.

This advice is easiest to apply at the interpersonal level. I knew the owners of a small firm that was facing a shrinking customer base in an unfavorable economy. They were looking to sell the business. The value of the business for a buyer wasn't significant, but they conceived of one way to maximize it. They contacted the owner of a competing firm who they well knew made decisions based on ego and characteristic insecurity. They had worked with him in the past and understood his motivations. They were able to get an amount several times over the value of their business in this acquisition by appealing to the competitor's ego and helping make him feel like a big shot.

> Hold out baits to entice the enemy. Feign disorder, and crush him.

The owners didn't seek to crush the competitor, but to sell their firm and move on to other pursuits. They sacrificed personal pride in stroking his ego, but in the end, they received more money than they would have otherwise and were able to tie a tidy bow on the business and that era of their careers. The better you know the enemy, the better you are able to give him the lure he will take.

PROTECT YOUR SECRETS

Keeping the enemy on the move also means shifting appearances to keep him guessing about your true next steps:

> By altering his arrangements and changing his plans, he keeps the enemy without definite knowledge. By shifting his camp and taking circuitous routes, he prevents the enemy from anticipating his purpose.

Salesforce CEO Marc Benioff clearly isn't afraid to antagonize the industry giants, including Microsoft, and keep them guessing as to his firm's next move. But when Microsoft shot back with its "I didn't get forced" Segway promotion at a Salesforce conference (using wordplay on its competitor's name), Salesforce responded as if it had been lying in wait for Microsoft's attack. When the adversary falls into your trap, even if it's a trap you construct seemingly on the fly, be ready to capture him. Sun Tzu's direction to use "a body of picked men" is instructive. An effort like this should only be left to the most conscientious, responsive, sharp players. Otherwise, it can't be trusted to be effective.

Don't allow adversaries to understand your plans or gain insight:

> On the day war is declared, close off all borders, destroy all passports, and do not allow their envoys to pass.[2]

Think about how your borders may be open to those seeking to gain intelligence for your competition. Are you vulnerable? Are your intellectual property, trade secrets are secret maneuvers at risk. If so, these mistakes could jeopardize your future.

> If a secret piece of news is divulged by a spy before the time is ripe, he must be put to death together with the man to whom the secret was told.

Okay, that may be a bit drastic for business. But the idea is important. Penalties for leaking information and violating the organization's trade secrets and inside information on movement should be severe. Short of putting traitors to death, all businesses, including small ones, should take the proper legal precautions. Nondisclosure agreements (NDAs) help protect your business's private information. NDAs establish confidential relationships with subcontractors, new employees, business partners, and anyone and everyone who has any behind-the-scenes access to any of your competitive information.

Noncompetes and nonsolicitation documents prohibit employees from leaving their jobs to start competing businesses. Depending on the agreement, it can also prevent employees from working for competing employers for a specific period of time.

Nonsolicitation agreements prevent employees from wooing away your customers for their own purposes. They may also restrict employees from soliciting coworkers from your company to join an employee's new competing venture. Consider all of these risks as you develop legal protection for your small business.

I worked with a small software development firm that either didn't have noncompetes in place or thought it would never need one for its all-star employee. This company didn't have a nonsolicitation with its clients to keep them from hiring away employees, either. Then, the inevitable happened. The company's largest client hired away its most talented software developer. This event was devastating to the young business, caused irreparable damage to the client relationship, and led to a steep reduction in the project value. These were dark days for that company. Learn from its very costly mistakes and have these agreements in place.

DIVIDE THE ENEMY

Unity, too, is an essential element for Sun Tzu. While you unite your forces, how can you divide your enemy's? By keeping him guessing as to where you'll fight next, you keep the adversary on the defensive:

> The spot where we intend to fight must not be made known; for then the enemy will have to prepare against a possible attack at several different points; and his forces being thus distributed in many directions, the numbers we shall have to face at any given point will be proportionately few.

Here again is the call to keep the enemy insecure about how, where, and when you'll strike:

Therefore, if we can make the enemy show his position while we are formless, we will be at full force while the enemy is divided.[3]

Formlessness is an advanced principle in some martial arts. Here again, we use water to connote suppleness and the ability to adapt to a situation. The goal is "flowing" with an attacker. Let me share an example.

My jujitsu instructor, Randy Hutchins, is a difficult person to put a joint lock on. He's mastered flowing so that locking him is like, well, locking water. Just when you think you have him, he relaxes whatever it is you think you have a good hold on, then he shifts and redirects. You end up on your posterior, generally accompanied by a significant amount of pain and, if you have a sense of irony, appreciation.

He's also a very difficult person to escape from, once he has a hold on you. I can counter joint locks from others, but from him, it's a whole different story. Until one day, when I nailed it. He had me in one of his famous wristlocks, when I surprised myself by finally doing what he'd been telling me to do, and relaxed and slipped out. It was effortless. Formless. Like water.

I was amazed. It worked! I think he was more pleased than surprised, as he had waited for me to finally "get" that concept. In a show of congratulations, he extended his hand. Thrilled with myself, I happily shook it. And he locked the [choose your expletive] out of me. It was priceless.

BE SELECTIVE

Hence he does not strive to ally himself with all and sundry, nor does he foster the power of other states. He carries out his own secret designs, keeping his antagonists in awe. Thus he is able to capture their cities and overthrow their kingdoms.

We discussed this passage in the study of building alliances in Chapter 6. But remember it, too, in the context of deception. In addition to choosing allies who play a clear role in your strategic objectives, you must be sure they are loyal. Be sure to remind them on an ongoing basis that you are a powerful partner, and working with you is very much in their best interests. Gaining strong allies to your side further helps keep antagonists in awe. But remember: Leveraging allies to dominate your market isn't about collecting partnership agreements or a batch of logos. If you share the same allies and partners with your competitors, how does that represent an advantage to your business?

INTELLIGENCE MUST ILLUMINATE MOVEMENT

Spies are indispensable resources for Sun Tzu:

> It is only the enlightened ruler and the wise general who will use the highest intelligence of the army for purposes of spying and thereby they achieve great results. Spies are a most important element in war, because on them depends an army's ability to move.

Let's look further at just how important this intelligence is. Sun Tzu says:

> What enables the wise sovereign and the good general to strike and conquer, and achieve things beyond the reach of ordinary men, is foreknowledge. Now this foreknowledge cannot be elicited from spirits; it cannot be obtained inductively from experience, nor by any deductive calculation. Knowledge of the enemy's dispositions can only be obtained from other men.

These "other men" are spies, "the most important element in war." Let's look at Sun Tzu's classifications of spies.

Types of Spies

Sun Tzu tells us of five types of spies:

> 1) Local spies; 2) inward spies; 3) converted spies; 4) doomed spies; 5) surviving spies.

Here, then, are Sun Tzu's descriptions of each of them, with commentary on the application to your business.

1. For local spies, we use the enemy's people.[4] They can be the employees of your competition who have little loyalty but useful information.

2. Having inward spies, making use of officials of the enemy. Officials can apply to executives and senior-level personnel. They can provide information publicly or privately, from unguarded conversations to statements they make in the press and social media.

3. Having converted spies, getting hold of the enemy's spies and using them for our own purposes. This description can apply to former employees and business partners of the competition. It can also describe friendly suppliers and vendors. But beware, naturally, that just as suppliers may share information with you, they may also share information with the competition. This is all the more reason to be selective: Choose reputable, high-integrity vendors and partners and treat them with dignity and honor.

Converted spies can lead to even more resources:

It is through the information brought by the converted spy that we are able to acquire and employ local and inward spies.

4. Having doomed spies, doing certain things openly for purposes of deception, and allowing our spies to know of them and report them to the enemy. Doomed spies are those who have no value to you and who you can't trust. They can be useful in carrying false signs to the enemy, which he can use to draw erroneous conclusions.

5. Surviving spies, finally, are those who bring back news from the enemy's camp. For your purposes, surviving spies are similar to local spies. The difference is that surviving spies are perhaps competitors' very poorly treated employees, or even vendors and partners, who will be highly motivated to share intelligence with you.

Remember always that the smart small-business leader is one who recognizes the value of having trusted friends, and who knows the cost of creating enemies.

Sun Tzu follows his descriptions of the five types of spies with this passage:

> Therefore, of those close to the army, none is closer than spies, no reward more generously given, and no matter in greater secrecy. Only the wisest ruler can use spies; only the most benevolent and upright general can use spies, and only the most alert and observant person can get the truth using spies.[5]

Clearly, intelligence gathering is serious business that requires secrecy, generosity, benevolence, and alertness. It also requires the ability to offer worthy rewards. Sun Tzu says you are wise to keep these informants close to you.

How to Treat "Spies"

Proper care and feeding of intelligence sources is essential for Sun Tzu:

> The enemy's spies who have come to spy on us must be sought out, tempted with bribes, led away and comfortably housed. Thus they will become converted spies and available for our service.

Sun Tzu calls for particularly generous care of converted spies:

> The end and aim of spying in all its five varieties is knowledge of the enemy; and this knowledge can only be derived, in the first instance, from the converted spy. Hence it is essential that the converted spy be treated with the utmost liberality.

PRACTICAL WAYS TO WIN WITH DECEPTION

There are a plethora of Sun Tzu–inspired methods that your small business can deploy to outmaneuver the competition. Here are some ideas you can consider adopting or enhancing:

Poach Salespeople

Hiring your competitors' salespeople is a smart way to gain intelligence about what they're selling and how they're positioning it. It's also a tool for capturing competitors' outstanding performers for your business's benefit. Jay Abraham has narrowed this idea down to a science. He says to determine your gross incremental profit for a first-time sale (i.e., profit before all amortized overhead) after hard direct expense. Then, once you know that number, go to your competitors' top salespeople. Offer to hire them and give them 100 percent of the profit (or more) for all new ac-counts they bring in, provided they switch employers and come to you, and stay for an agreed-on period.[6]

Felix Dennis has said he's never known a single person in a rival organization, even one well paid and cared for, who wouldn't meet him for a quiet drink after hours. He put these meetings to very good use. "I've discovered more about what rivals have been up to in this manner than any other. And I poached the good ones," he said in his autobiography.[7]

Get Chummy with Prospects

If your customers like you, and especially if they don't like or respect your competitors, they'll show you your adversary's sales materials, presentations, and even proposals. It is ethical? It de-pends on who you ask. Are penalties against this practice en-forceable? Probably not.

Gather intelligence in pitch meetings, too. Find out who you're up against, and as much as you can about how they're selling against you. Again, if your prospects like you better than the other candidates, you'll be surprised how much they may share with you. I frequently have been.

Find Out Why You Win and Why You Lose

When you win find out why. What was it about you that stood out above the competitors? Why does the customer think you're the superior choice? Be careful here: The question isn't why you think you're the superior choice. It's why the customer says they think you are.

And while it's less enjoyable, when you lose, it's just as im-portant to find out why. It may even be *more* important to find out why you lost than why you won. I'm consistently surprised at the number of sales professionals who don't ask about the businesses they're up against and the players they lose to. The worst thing your prospects can tell you is that they won't tell you. But if you ask the right questions the right way, you stand to gain high-value intelligence. Relationships are everything. Consider taking key would-be clients out to lunch or drinks to get the most information, even for business that you lose. People are much more forthcoming in settings outside of the office and after one simple drink.

Do a lost-case analysis. When you lose customers, don't simply turn inward and listen to what your team tells you. There are almost always far too many assumptions here. To find out why you lost customers, you should have an independent party conduct a study so that you can get to the real reasons. Taking this step is virtually guaranteed to illuminate some weaknesses in your organization of which you're probably completely unaware. It's more costly not to do this analysis than to do it.

Track the Press

Keeping tabs on known competitors and learning about newcomers through the media is nothing new. Long before search engines ruled the day, companies would hire clipping services to track the press. Today, it's easier than ever to get access to media stories, but with the myriad business media outlets available, it's difficult to digest all the information you find. Set up Google Alerts for your business, your key competitors, customers, and other market keywords. If you're in a competitive space and need to monitor players, include local business journals and dailies from your competitors' regions. Companies may be less guarded in what they say to their local reporters than they would be with a national trade outlet or high circulation daily.

Probe at Trade Shows

Trade shows are an exceptional way to generate leads. But what small businesses often don't fully appreciate is that shows are also an outstanding way to gain intelligence. You can send employees and even business partners, allies, and customers to listen in on booth chatter and watch demos. The wife of the CEO of a health IT company I worked with is a nurse. She went to many industry trade shows to gather intelligence from competitors, and, as a nurse, she had unfettered access to competitors' unguarded sales pitches. Be sure your "spies" are equipped with the right questions to gain useful intelligence, and that they don't simply come back with the same brochures everyone else gets.

Get on Their Mailing List

Join your competitors' mailing lists so that you'll know of news and product announcements. Sign up for webinars and download white papers and demos to gather as much information on the competition as possible. Because of the actions of competitors, I always suggest that companies make access to substantive information permission-based so that you can at least attempt to screen out rivals.

Shop for Their Secrets

If your competitor is in retail sales with a physical location, you should make it a point to have an employee or hired gun walk the aisles and observe as much as possible about the facility, its customers, and its staff. You can call the company's order and support lines and evaluate the strength of their customer service. You can hire a mystery shopping firm, too, to pretend to be a prospect. I'm not a big fan of this tactic since it's openly dishonest, but it's also pretty common practice. You should be aware that it's done and remain vigilant against it in your small business.

Five Guys uses a smart way to shop for secrets—within its own business. The restaurant chain conducts audits of each store, every week. A secret shopper goes in, under the guise of a customer, and rates the crew on bathroom cleanliness, courtesy, and food preparation. Unlike secret shopping of competitors, this is fair game. Employees are aware of the policy, which is used to keep them sharp and to contribute to a culture of exceptional service. Winning crews are incentivized with cash rewards. CEO Jerry Murrell said the company pays as much as $12 million out annually to winners of these inspections.[8] If you see this as a cost, your thinking is limited.

Google for Hidden Pages

You know to search public places online for information on your competitors. But do you know about the hidden pages you can find? Google searches by file format (filetype:doc, or pdf, xls, and ppt) and site or domain searches (site:companyname) can uncover data or presentations. Competitors or others who have these resources may post them to a link they believe is hidden, and may even forget about them.[9]

Pay Attention to Social Media

This effort can be more than a little tedious, but there may also be a wealth of valuable information about your competitors' people on social networks. It's possible that a competitor may have one or two key salespeople who are particularly chatty. Salespeople also like to share their excitement over hot leads and new customers, hoping this spirit is contagious. They may brag about new wins or upcoming pitch meetings, or otherwise give clues as to who they're selling to on their personal social media sites. Yes, it takes a while to mine this data, but under the right set of circumstances it can uncover gold.

Use social media to engage customers and gain intelligence. Go beyond the transaction and truly involve your customers. The dominant player in your market may spend a lot of money on think tanks, focus groups, and other studies. You can reap similar gains, but at a much lower cost than your big-budget adversaries. Instead of incurring that hefty price tag, build a successful social media presence. You can then have thousands of people willing to tell you exactly what they want and why they will buy it from you, as you grow your audience. How are you leveraging these channels to gain intelligence for your small business?

Scan Their Job Ads

Online job aggregators are excellent places to keep tabs on your competitors' hiring requirements. Watch the skills a company may be hiring for, and you can see what new initiatives may be coming. Of course, you can check your competitors' websites too, but they may be less public about strategic changes.

5-HOUR ENERGY

Some time ago I received an e-mail from my colleague at Sun Tzu Strategies, Mark McNeilly, with a link to an article on Manoj Bhargava, the founder of 5-Hour Energy. That link was to a *Forbes* piece by Clare O'Connor that, until that point, was the most substantive public information on Bhargava. The entrepreneur does few interviews and remains somewhat enigmatic. (On the basis of that one interview, many other articles on him were written.) Mark was intrigued by how much this monk-turned-businessman exemplified many characteristics of Sun Tzu. He got our attention.

As noted in Chapter 9, "Focus," 5-Hour Energy is a picture of many principles of Sun Tzu. The company took the less direct route in creating a new category with its energy shot, rather than competing for fridge space with Coke, Pepsi, and Red Bull. It shut down rivals completely and has driven some of them out of business. Also-rans like 6-Hour Power and 8-Hour Energy have been sued or otherwise knocked out of the market by lawyers at Living Essentials, the parent company of 5-Hour Energy.

But it may be under the (ethical) deception banner where Sun Tzu is seen most vividly. Throughout the rise in popularity of the product, Bhargava stayed under the radar. He was a mystery. He barely registered on web searches. He was able to make his moves without drawing attention from competitors large or small.[10]

Despite the illustration of deception, the customer is the last person Bhargava, or any other intelligent business person, wants to deceive. As he told O'Connor in that *Forbes* article, "It's not the little bottle. It's not the placement. It's the product. You can con people one time, but nobody pays $3 twice."

iGATE

Sun Tzu writes of how a wise general will turn disadvantage to advantage. But Phaneesh Murthy, founder and former CEO of iGATE, took it one step further. Like Netflix did to Blockbuster, he turned his competitors' advantages to their disadvantage. Headquartered in Silicon Valley, iGATE is an Indian-owned IT firm that has grown to $1 billion in revenue from $300 million in under five year. It's regularly lauded as one of the best Indian companies to work for. As Murthy told Kaihan Krippendorff, author of *The Way of Innovation*, he came from Infosys, one of two firms that transformed India into the IT outsourcing powerhouse that it is today. Infosys did it by taking what competitors saw as an asset and turning it against them. The big-tech consulting giants saw their legions of consultants as their top advantage. However, Infosys transformed how software is built and opened the door to an entirely new consulting model.[11]

Murthy applied that same pattern at iGATE and turned the advantage of that firm's competitors upside down as well. Peers, including his former employer, have legions of developers. Murthy turned this perceived asset into an opportunity for iGATE. The idea he put forth was to learn each customer's business so that iGATE can make improvements unlike any traditional IT company. For example, iGATE applied this logic to consumer loans, which are typically done manually by highly skilled underwriters. iGATE demonstrated that the underwriters could be replaced with a set of rules that reduced loan approval turnaround time from forty to seventeen days, on average.[12]

Unlike almost every other IT consulting firm, iGATE doesn't charge by the hour. This model, said Murthy, brings with it "diametrically opposed objectives . . . the customer always wants to reduce and company wants to increase." I can attest to this paradoxical reality, because my own business is based in Washington, DC, the consulting capital of the world (or at least a healthy territory). Instead, iGATE bills for performance.[13]

15

SUN TZU AND THE FUTURE OF YOUR BUSINESS

Now that you've studied the twelve key attributes, here's the question you should ask yourself: If Sun Tzu were running your small business, what would he do differently to bring it into accord with his battlefield strategy?

The spirit of Sun Tzu will be within you if you pose this question to yourself. Take these principles to heart and use them to defeat even your biggest competitors. How will you use *The Art of War* to dominate your market?

KEY THEMES FROM *THE ART OF WAR*

Here is a summary of Sun Tzu's fundamental principles that apply to small business. Use them as an ongoing reference your business:

Acquire a comprehensive understanding. A full understanding of your organization's weaknesses and strengths, in relationship to your competition, is a requirement for Sun Tzu. This is an ongoing effort that demands constant vigilance.

Build alliances. Think about your community and influencers, everyone from partners to employees, customers, vendors and suppliers, investors, and friends. Your strength will be a sum of these parts. To dominate, you need to leverage these combined forces. Again I say, small-business leaders need all the friends we can get.

Secure your position. To win, your business must take the most advantageous position. For Sun Tzu, a good position is high ground, on a sunny spot, with the supply line that is well guarded. Choose your ground carefully and consider every detail great and small.

Control perceptions. Small businesses have many opportunities to shape how they are viewed by customers, partners, and the rest of the world. While you may opt to deceive the enemy and shape appearances to advance your position, be sure that you're also directing what your customers and allies see, hear, and know about you so that you can position your business as favorably as possible. Every single engagement your customer has with your company counts.

Think growth. Successful business leaders know that they can't expect to achieve aggressive growth goals if they simply opt to hold ground. Always think growth, not just taking a defensive position.

Play the long game. Strategy is framed by the big picture. It is an endurance race. Don't let your business slip into sacrificing long-term objectives for short-term benefits.

Be prepared to turn disadvantage to advantage. The seeds of opportunity are in disadvantage. But you must be prepared to seize these opportunities.

Win first. This quintessential Sun Tzu concept is not to be taken for granted. It's one of the most important ideas from all of *The Art of War.*

Act decisively. While gathering intelligence and carefully planning every tactic around your strategic objectives is essential, it's also fundamental to make informed decisions, and move quickly and with conviction when the time is right.

Using the few, out-strategize the many. The only way to take on and defeat the big competitors is to do so with superior strategy. In one well-executed battle at a time, Sun Tzu used a smaller number to defeat a larger force, and you must do the same.

Fight only when necessary. War is an incredible drain on resources, including human resources. Remember that the best way is to attack the enemy's strategy, followed by disrupting his alliances.

Time your attacks. Part of knowing your adversary and knowing the strength of your organization is knowing when conditions are most appropriate for an attack. A poorly timed concept won't reach its full potential.

Make use of the unexpected. Keep your competitors in the dark so that they won't know what to expect from you or when. The unexpected is a powerful weapon that keeps adversaries wholly unprepared. Keep the enemy on the move.

Go where the enemy isn't. Remember (always!) Sun Tzu's direction to avoid attacking a larger adversary on his terms. Niches are small but specific and well-defined segments of buyers. You don't have to "find" a niche. You can create one, like Elmer T. Lee did with premium bourbon. Go where the enemy isn't and identify needs and wants that aren't being satisfied.

Attack their weak spots relentlessly. Large organizations are typically prepared to counter direct competition, but they are woefully unprepared to respond to guerilla insurgencies. How can you hone in on your big competitors' weaknesses?

Create unity. Present a unified, consistent image and brand experience and you'll be ahead of much of the competition. Work to maintain unity, too.

Miss no opportunity to defeat the enemy. If you're going to defeat the competition and dominate your market, you must take advantage of every single opportunity.

Adapt to trends and vary your plans. Identify and follow the trends in your industry. Vary your plans accordingly. Don't fight it. Tablet and smartphone sales were escalating as DVD player sales were leveling. Netflix followed the trend instead of trying to capture a model with waning demand.

Execute flawlessly. The success of every strategy comes down to one essential thing: execution. Once you've defined yourself, you have to deliver the goods repeatedly and relentlessly. There are no days off.

Turn devious to direct. Outplay your adversaries so that they will have to take the longer, circuitous way, and you will get to the destination sooner.

Maximize resources. Make the best use of the comparatively limited resources you have. And don't focus so much on acquiring new customers that you forget to maximize your current customers. Take advantage of the opportunities in leveling the playing field posed by the Internet, social media, and a global workforce.

BONUS SUN TZU PRINCIPLES

While not expressly covered in Sun Tzu's 2,500-year-old Chinese battlefield strategy, these principles are in concert with his direction. If Sun Tzu were developing strategy for your small business, he'd recommend these two bonus principles:

Differentiate yourself. Most small-business owners may intellectually understand the importance of differentiating themselves, yet many aren't able to execute this strategy in a way that makes a real distinction in the marketplace. For examples of how to differentiate successfully, look to 5-Hour Energy, which created the bold new category of energy shots. And while Five Guys didn't create the "better burger" category, it created a stand-out brand by combining an aggressive franchise strategy with a commitment to quality control, never using frozen ingredients, rewarding employees for performance, and offering a limited menu of items done consistently well.

Safeguard every customer interaction. Every single encounter that a customer has with your company is what ultimately makes up your brand. How you are perceived is everything. You need to occupy prime real estate inside the brain of your customers, your business partners, and potential employees. Your goal should be to have legions of loyal customers who comprise a powerful community. Think of the community of users who turned to and promoted PayPal, paving the way for that business to explode. Remember how Zappos leverages a cadre of committed employees to build extremely loyal customers. How can you build a powerful community for your small business?

APPENDIX: KEY SUN TZU PASSAGES FOR SMALL BUSINESS

*T*he *Art of War* in its entirety is both useful and meaningful for small businesses. Below, however, are excerpts that are particularly impactful for small-business leaders looking to dominate their markets. Refer back to them frequently for a strategic sanity check.

> Standing on the defensive indicates insufficient strength; attacking, a superabundance of strength.

> The best policy in war is to attack the enemy's strategy. The second best way is to disrupt his alliances through diplomatic means. The next best method is to attack his army in the field. The worst policy is to attack walled cities. Attacking cities is the last resort when there is no alternative.[1]

Numerical weakness comes from having to prepare against possible attacks; numerical strength, from compelling our adversary to make these preparations against us.

You may advance and be absolutely irresistible, if you make for the enemy's weak points; you may retire and be safe from pursuit if your movements are more rapid than those of the enemy.

When a general, unable to estimate the enemy's strength, allows an inferior force to engage a larger one, or hurls a weak detachment against a powerful one, and neglects to place picked soldiers in the front rank, the result must be rout.

The control of a large force is the same principle as the control of a few men: it is merely a question of dividing up their numbers.

If, on the other hand, in the midst of difficulties we are always ready to seize an advantage, we may extricate ourselves from misfortune.

For it is precisely when a force has fallen into harm's way that is capable of striking a blow for victory.

We can form a single united body, while the enemy must split up into fractions. Hence there will be a whole pitted against separate parts of a whole, which means that we shall be many to the enemy's few.

Question: If the enemy is numerous and is advancing in well-ordered arrays, how are they handled?

 Answer: First seize what they care about and they will do as wished.[2]

If less in number, be capable of defending yourself. And if in all respects unfavorable, be capable of eluding [the enemy]. Hence, a weak force will eventually fall captive to a strong one if it simply holds ground and conducts a desperate defense.[3]

Be flexible and decide your line of action according to the situation on the enemy side.[4]

NOTES

CHAPTER 1: ABOUT SUN TZU AND *THE ART OF WAR*

1. Thomas Huynh, *The Art of War—Spirituality for Conflict: Annotated and Explained* (Woodstock, VT: SkyLight Paths Publishing, 2012), xxx.
2. J. H. Huang, *Sun-Tzu: The Art of War—The New Translation* (New York: William Morrow, 1993), 17–18.
3. Huang, *Art of War—The New Translation*, 18–19.
4. Ibid.
5. Ibid, 15.
6. Mark R. McNeilly, *Sun Tzu and the Art of Modern Warfare* (New York: Oxford University Press, 2001), 6–7.

CHAPTER 2: THE POWER OF APPLYING *THE ART OF WAR*
FOR *SMALL BUSINESS*

1. Thomas Huynh, *The Art of War—Spirituality for Conflict: Annotated and Explained* (Woodstock, VT: SkyLight Paths Publishing, 2012), xxvi.
2. Marc Benioff, foreword to *The Art of War—Spirituality for Conflict: Annotated and Explained* (Woodstock, VT: SkyLight Paths Publishing, 2012), ix.
3. Devon Pendleton, "Hidden Chobani Billionaire Emerges as Greek Yogurt Soars," *Bloomberg,* September 14, 2012.
4. Dinah Eng, "How We Got Started: Jim Koch: Samuel Adams's Beer Revolutionary," *CNN Money,* March 21, 2013.
5. Marla Tabaka, "5 Tactics to Conquer Goliath Competitors," *Inc.,* April 9, 2012.
6. Felix Dennis, *How to Get Rich: The Distilled Wisdom of One of Britain's Wealthiest Self-Made Entrepreneurs* (London: Ebury Press, 2007), 234.

7. Nadia Goodman, "James Dyson on Using Failure to Drive Success," *Entrepreneur,* November 5, 2012.

8. Scott Maxwell, "Small Business Innovation Lessons from Salesforce.com," *Open-View Labs Blog,* January 31, 2013.

9. Steve Denning, "Clayton Christensen and the Innovators' Smackdown," *Forbes,* April 5, 2012.

10. IBIS World, *Business Coaching in the U.S.: Market Research Report,* November 2013.

11. Mark R. McNeilly, *Sun Tzu and the Art of Modern Warfare* (New York: Oxford University Press, 2001).

CHAPTER 3: UNDERSTAND YOURSELF

1. Sylvie Leotin, "Atari: The Original Lean Startup," *VentureBeat,* October 13, 2010.

2. Bill Taylor, "Why Zappos Pays New Employees to Quit—and You Should Too," *HBR Blog Network,* May 19, 2008.

3. "Frequently Asked Questions," Zappos Insights corporate website, www.zapposinsights.com/about/faqs#q5.

4. Dinah Eng, "How We Got Started: Jim Koch: Samuel Adams's Beer Revolutionary," *CNN Money,* March 21, 2013.

5. Liz Welch, "How I Did It: Jerry Murrell, Five Guys Burgers and Fries," *Inc.,* April 1, 2010.

6. Monte Burke, "Five Guys Burgers: America's Fastest Growing Restaurant Chain," *Forbes,* July 18, 2012.

7. Burke, "Five Guys Burgers."

8. Ibid.

9. Welch, "How I Did It: Jerry Murrell, Five Guys Burgers and Fries."

10. Ibid.

11. Burke, "Five Guys Burgers."

12. Eng, "How We Got Started: Jim Koch."

13. Ibid.

14. Ibid.

15. Ibid.

CHAPTER 4: UNDERSTAND THE ENEMY

1. Gerald A. Michaelson and Steven Michaelson, *The Art of War for Managers: 5 Strategic Rules* (Avon, MA: Adams Media, 2010), 121.

2. J. H. Huang, *Sun-Tzu: The Art of War—The New Translation* (New York: William Morrow, 1993), 91.

3. Huang, *Sun-Tzu: The Art of War—The New Translation,* 160.

4. Daniel Gross, "It's All Greek to Him: Chobani's Unlikely Success Story," *The Daily Beast,* June 12, 2013.

5. Gross, "It's All Greek to Him: Chobani's Unlikely Success Story."

6. Devon Pendleton, "Hidden Chobani Billionaire Emerges as Greek Yogurt Soars," *Bloomberg,* September 14, 2012.

7. Maria Bartiromo, "Bartiromo: Chobani CEO at Center of Greek Yogurt Craze," *USA Today,* June 16, 2013.

8. Bryan Gruley, "At Chobani, the Turkish King of Greek Yogurt," *Businessweek,* January 31, 2013.

9. Pendleton, "Hidden Chobani Billionaire Emerges as Greek Yogurt Soars."

10. Ibid.

11. Ibid.

12. Ibid.

CHAPTER 5: UNDERSTAND THE MARKET

1. Dinah Eng, "How We Got Started: Jim Koch: Samuel Adams's Beer Revolutionary," *CNN Money,* March 21, 2013.

2. James Duval, "Secrets of Success: How Cisco Outlasted Its Competitors," *CustomerTHINK Blog,* June 3, 2013

3. Jay Abraham, *The Sticking Point Solution: 9 Ways to Move Your Business from Stagnation to Stunning Growth in Tough Economic Times.* (New York: Vanguard Press, 2009), 24.

4. Andy Sambidge, "Yahoo!'s Maktoob Deal Valued at $175m—Report," *ArabianBusiness.com,* September 10, 2009.

5. Thomas Huynh, *The Art of War—Spirituality for Conflict: Annotated and Explained* (Woodstock, VT: SkyLight Paths Publishing, 2012), 135.

6. Malcolm Gladwell, *The Tipping Point: How Little Things Can Make a Big Difference* (New York: Little, Brown, 2002), 193–200.

7. Gladwell, *The Tipping Point,* 206–213.

8. Ibid, 213–215.

9. Ibid.

10. Kathryn Quinn Thomas, "Golisano Built Paychex into a Success Story," *Rochester Business Journal,* October 8, 2004.

CHAPTER 6: SUN TZU FOR CUSTOMERS
AND BUSINESS ALLIANCES

1. "Interview with Marc Benioff," *Sonshi.com.*

2. Joe Calloway, *Becoming a Category of One: How Extraordinary Companies Transcend Commodity and Defy Comparison* (Hoboken, NJ: John Wiley & Sons, 2009), xii.

3. Mark Caro, "Charlie Trotter Preaches Excellence to the Extreme," *Chicago Tribune,* August 28, 2012.

4. Sylvie Leotin, "Atari: The Original Lean Startup," *VentureBeat,* October 13, 2010.

5. John R. Harbison, Peter Pekar Jr., Albert Viscio, and David Maloney, *The Allianced Enterprise: Breakout Strategy for the New Millennium* (Los Angeles: Booz Allen & Hamilton, 2000).

6. "Interview Transcript: Meg Whitman, Ebay," *Financial Times,* June 18, 2006.

7. Mark R. McNeilly, *Sun Tzu and the Art of Modern Warfare* (New York: Oxford University Press, 2001), 34.

8. Dana McMahan, "Craft Distillers Breaking into Kentucky's Billion-Dollar Bourbon Industry," *NBC News,* August 30, 2013.

9. Paul Vitello, "Elmer T. Lee, Whose Premium Bourbon Revived an Industry, Dies at 93," *New York Times,* July 21, 2013.

10. Vitello, "Elmer T. Lee."

11. Jay Abraham, *The Sticking Point Solution* (New York: Vanguard Press, 2009), 71.

12. Abraham, *The Sticking Point Solution,* 94.

13. Ibid.

14. Max Nisen and Alexandra Mondalek, "Invaluable Advice from 18 of America's Top Small Business Owners," *Business Insider,* June 21, 2013.

15. Sean O'Hagan, "The Nine Lives of Felix Dennis," *The Guardian,* June 1, 2013.

16. Felix Dennis, *How to Get Rich: The Distilled Wisdom of One of Britain's Wealthiest Self-Made Entrepreneurs* (London: Ebury Press, 2007), 84–86.

17. Ibid.

18. Ibid.

19. Ibid.

20. CRDF Global, "GIST TechConnect Ideation," online panel discussion January 23, 2013.

21. CRDF Global.

CHAPTER 7: EMBODY THE GENERAL

1. J. H. Huang, *Sun-Tzu: The Art of War—The New Translation* (New York: William Morrow, 1993), 131–132.

2. Monte Burke, "Five Guys Burgers: America's Fastest Growing Restaurant Chain," *Forbes,* July 18, 2012.

3. Max Nisen and Alexandra Mondalek, "Invaluable Advice from 18 of America's Top Small Business Owners," *Business Insider,* June 21, 2013.

4. Thomas Huynh, *The Art of War—Spirituality for Conflict: Annotated and Explained* (Woodstock, VT: SkyLight Paths Publishing, 2012), 166.

5. Huang, *Sun-Tzu: The Art of War—The New Translation,* 230–231.

6. Adam Bryant, "Finding Purpose in Tunneling Through Granite," *New York Times,* April 13, 2013.

7. Huang, *Sun-Tzu: The Art of War—The New Translation,* 112.

8. Huynh, *The Art of War—Spirituality for Conflict: Annotated and Explained,* 93.

CHAPTER 8: PERSEVERANCE

1. Max Nisen and Alexandra Mondalek, "Invaluable Advice from 18 of America's Top Small Business Owners," *Business Insider,* June 21, 2013.

2. Jay Abraham, *The Sticking Point Solution: 9 Ways to Move Your Business from Stagnation to Stunning Growth in Tough Economic Times* (New York: Vanguard Press, 2009), 5–6.

3. Adam Bryant, "Finding Purpose in Tunneling Through Granite," *New York Times,* April 13, 2013.

4. Bryant, "Finding Purpose in Tunneling Through Granite."

5. Felix Dennis, *How to Get Rich: The Distilled Wisdom of One of Britain's Wealthiest Self-Made Entrepreneurs* (London: Ebury Press, 2007), 234.

6. Dennis, *How to Get Rich.*

7. Thomas Huynh, *The Art of War—Spirituality for Conflict: Annotated and Explained* (Woodstock, VT: SkyLight Paths Publishing, 2012), 73.

8. Chuck Salter, "Failure Doesn't Suck," *Fast Company,* April 10, 2007.
9. Episode 29, "The Red Dot," *Seinfeld,* NBC, December 11, 1991. www.seinfeld-scripts.com/TheRedDot.htm.
10. Salter, "Failure Doesn't Suck."
11. Margaret Heffernan, "James Dyson on Creating a Vacuum That Actually, Well, Sucks," *Reader's Digest,* February 2009.
12. Nadia Goodman, "James Dyson on Using Failure to Drive Success," *Entrepreneur,* November 5, 2012.
13. "Vacuum Makers Dyson, Hoover Settle Lawsuit," *Appliance Magazine,* October 10, 2002.
14. Jon Birger, "How Jeffery Boyd Took Priceline from Dot-Bomb to Highflier," *CNN Money,* September 11, 2012.
15. Birger, "How Jeffery Boyd Took Priceline from Dot-Bomb to Highflier."
16. Ibid.

CHAPTER 9: FOCUS

1. Mark R. McNeilly, *Sun Tzu and the Art of Modern Warfare* (New York: Oxford University Press, 2001), 71–72.
2. Gerald A. Michaelson and Steven Michaelson, *The Art of War for Managers: 5 Strategic Rules* (Avon, MA: Adams Media, 2010), 138.
3. J. H. Huang, *Sun-Tzu: The Art of War—The New Translation* (New York: William Morrow, 1993), 71.
4. Thomas Huynh, *The Art of War—Spirituality for Conflict: Annotated and Explained* (Woodstock, VT: SkyLight Paths Publishing, 2012), 97.
5. "Vacuum Makers Dyson, Hoover Settle Lawsuit," *Appliance Magazine,* October 10, 2002.
6. Dinah Eng, "How We Got Started: Jim Koch: Samuel Adams's Beer Revolutionary," *CNN Money,* March 21, 2013.
7. Burt Helm, "How I Did It: James Dyson," *Inc.,* February 28, 2012.
8. Eng, "How We Got Started: Jim Koch."
9. Elizabeth Heubeck, "Wegmans' Grocery List for Success," *Baltimore Business Journal,* March 20, 2013.
10. Daniel Duggan, "Manoj Bhargava on What Makes Successes Like 5-Hour Energy: Don't Waste Your Energy," *Crain's Detroit Business,* May 21, 2012.
11. Duggan, "Manoj Bhargava on What Makes Successes Like 5-Hour Energy."
12. Welch, "How I Did It: Jerry Murrell, Five Guys Burgers and Fries."
13. Monte Burke, "Five Guys Burgers: America's Fastest Growing Restaurant Chain," *Forbes,* July 18, 2012.
14. Burke, "Five Guys Burgers: America's Fastest Growing Restaurant Chain."

CHAPTER 10: UNITY

1. Joe Calloway, *Becoming a Category of One: How Extraordinary Companies Transcend Commodity and Defy Comparison* (Hoboken, NJ: John Wiley, 2009), xi.
2. Dinah Eng, "How We Got Started: Jim Koch: Samuel Adams's Beer Revolutionary," *CNN Money,* March 21, 2013.

3. Tony Hsieh, *Delivering Happiness* (New York: Hachette Book Group, 2010).
4. Tony Hsieh, "Your Culture Is Your Brand," *Zappos Blogs: CEO and COO Blog,* January 3, 2009.
5. Hsieh, "Your Culture Is Your Brand."
6. Thomas Huynh, *The Art of War—Spirituality for Conflict: Annotated and Explained* (Woodstock, VT: SkyLight Paths Publishing, 2012), 93.
7. Huynh, *The Art of War—Spirituality for Conflict,* 157.
8. Elizabeth Heubeck, "Wegmans' Grocery List for Success," *Baltimore Business Journal,* March 20, 2013.
9. Heubeck, "Wegmans' Grocery List for Success."
10. Ibid.
11. David Rohde, "The Anti-Walmart: The Secret Sauce of Wegmans Is People," *The Atlantic,* March 23, 2012.
12. Heubeck, "Wegmans' Grocery List for Success."
13. Ibid.
14. "Interview with Marc Benioff," *Sonshi.com.*
15. Ibid.
16. Ibid.
17. Huynh, *The Art of War—Spirituality for Conflict,* x.

CHAPTER 11: MANEUVERING

1. Gerald A. Michaelson and Steven Michaelson, *The Art of War for Managers: 5 Strategic Rules* (Avon, MA: Adams Media, 2010), 25.
2. Thomas Huynh, *The Art of War—Spirituality for Conflict: Annotated and Explained* (Woodstock, VT: SkyLight Paths Publishing, 2012), p. 85.
3. J. H. Huang, *Sun-Tzu: The Art of War—The New Translation* (New York: William Morrow, 1993), 96.
4. Ben Parr, "Here's Why Amazon Bought Zappos," *Mashable,* July 22, 2009.
5. Parr, "Here's Why Amazon Bought Zappos."
6. Michaelson and Michaelson, *The Art of War for Managers: 5 Strategic Rules,* 121.
7. Pascal-Emmanuel Gobry, "10 Brilliant Startups That Failed Because They Were Ahead of Their Time," *Business Insider,* May 4, 2011.
8. *Funding Universe,* "Ask Jeeves, Inc. History."
9. Gobry, "10 Brilliant Startups That Failed Because They Were Ahead of Their Time."
10. Ibid.
11. Ibid.
12. Michaelson and Michaelson, *The Art of War for Managers: 5 Strategic Rules,* 27.
13. Sarah Green, "Who New CEOs Fire First," *HBR Blog Network,* July 8, 2013.
14. Alyssa Abkowitz, "How Netflix Got Started," *CNN Money,* January 28, 2009.
15. Adam Hartung, "Netflix—The Turnaround Story of 2012!" *Forbes,* January 29, 2013.
16. Hartung, "Netflix—The Turnaround Story of 2012!"
17. Ibid.
18. Michaelson and Michaelson, *The Art of War for Managers: 5 Strategic Rules,* 27.

CHAPTER 12: ADAPTATION

1. Gerald A. Michaelson and Steven Michaelson, *The Art of War for Managers: 5 Strategic Rules* (Avon, MA: Adams Media, 2010), 56.
2. Ilya Pozin, "9 Biggest Mistakes New Entrepreneurs Make," *Inc.*, July 20, 2013.
3. Michaelson and Michaelson, *The Art of War for Managers: 5 Strategic Rules*, 36.
4. Joe Calloway, *Becoming a Category of One: How Extraordinary Companies Transcend Commodity and Defy Comparison* (Hoboken, NJ: John Wiley, 2009), 236.
5. Clayton Christensen, "Disruptive Innovation," Claytonchristensen.com.
6. Christensen, "Disruptive Innovation."
7. Steve Denning, "Clayton Christensen and the Innovators' Smackdown," *Forbes*, April 5, 2012.
8. Andrew Keen, "Keen On ... Clay Christensen: How to Escape the Innovator's Dilemma [TCTV]," video interview, *TechCrunch*, April 2, 2012.
9. Denning, "Clayton Christensen and the Innovators' Smackdown."
10. Adam L. Penenberg, "Reid Hoffman on PayPal's Pivoted Path to Success," *Fast Company*, August 9, 2012.
11. Penenberg, "Reid Hoffman on PayPal's Pivoted Path to Success."
12. *Funding Universe*, "Priceline.com Incorporated History."
13. *Funding Universe*, "Priceline.com."
14. Ibid.
15. Jon Birger, "How Jeffery Boyd Took Priceline from Dot-Bomb to Highflier," *CNN Money*, September 11, 2012.

CHAPTER 13: SPIRIT

1. J. H. Huang, *Sun-Tzu: The Art of War—The New Translation* (New York: William Morrow, 1993), 191.
2. Huang, *Sun-Tzu: The Art of War—The New Translation*, 73.
3. Thomas Huynh, *The Art of War—Spirituality for Conflict: Annotated and Explained* (Woodstock, VT: SkyLight Paths Publishing, 2012), x.
4. Julie Bort, "Our Favorite Crazy Stunts from Salesforce Leader Marc Benioff," *Business Insider*, March 15, 2012.
5. Marc Benioff, foreword to *The Art of War—Spirituality for Conflict: Annotated and Explained* (Woodstock, VT: SkyLight Paths Publishing), xii.
6. Bort, "Our Favorite Crazy Stunts from Salesforce Leader Marc Benioff."
7. Ibid.
8. Ibid.
9. MarketWatch commentary, "Salesforce CEO Pulls Off Excellent Stunt," *MarketWatch*, October 5, 2011.
10. Benioff, foreword to *The Art of War—Spirituality for Conflict*, xii.

CHAPTER 14: DECEPTION

1. Jay Abraham, *The Sticking Point Solution: 9 Ways to Move Your Business from Stagnation to Stunning Growth in Tough Economic Times* (New York: Vanguard Press, 2009), 131–132.

2. Thomas Huynh, *The Art of War—Spirituality for Conflict: Annotated and Explained* (Woodstock, VT: SkyLight Paths Publishing, 2012), 177.

3. Huynh, *The Art of War—Spirituality for Conflict: Annotated and Explained*, 73.

4. Ibid., 193.

5. Ibid., 195.

6. Abraham, *The Sticking Point Solution*, 250.

7. Felix Dennis, *How to Get Rich: The Distilled Wisdom of One of Britain's Wealthiest Self-Made Entrepreneurs* (London: Ebury Press, 2007), 236.

8. Liz Welch, "How I Did It: Jerry Murrell, Five Guys Burgers and Fries," *Inc.*, April 1, 2010.

9. Carol Tice, "12 Ways to (Legally) Spy on Your Competitors," *Entrepreneur*, November 17, 2011.

10. Clare O'Connor, "The Mystery Monk Making Billions with 5-Hour Energy," *Forbes*, February 8, 2012.

11. Kaihan Krippendorff, "How Great Entrepreneurs Lure Their Competitors' Sheep Away," *Fast Company*, May 16, 2012.

12. Krippendorff, "How Great Entrepreneurs Lure Their Competitors' Sheep Away."

13. Ibid.

APPENDIX: KEY SUN TZU PASSAGES FOR SMALL BUSINESS

1. Gerald A. Michaelson and Steven Michaelson, *The Art of War for Managers: 5 Strategic Rules* (Avon, MA: Adams Media, 2010), 25.

2. J. H. Huang, *Sun-Tzu: The Art of War—The New Translation* (New York: William Morrow, 1993), 96.

3. Michaelson and Michaelson, *The Art of War for Managers: 5 Strategic Rules*, 27.

4. Ibid., 56

BIBLIOGRAPHY

Abkowitz, Alyssa. "How Netflix Got Started." *CNN Money,* January 28, 2009. money.cnn.com/2009/01/27/news/newsmakers/hastings_netflix.fortune/.

Abraham, Jay. *The Sticking Point Solution: 9 Ways to Move Your Business from Stagnation to Stunning Growth in Tough Economic Times.* New York: Vanguard Press, 2009.

Bartiromo, Maria. "Bartiromo: Chobani CEO at Center of Greek Yogurt Craze." *USA Today,* June 16, 2013. www.usatoday.com/story/money/columnist/bartiromo/2013/06/16/chobani-ulukaya-yogurt/2423611/.

Benioff, Marc. Foreword to *The Art of War—Spirituality for Conflict: Annotated and Explained.* Woodstock, VT: SkyLight Paths Publishing, 2012.

Birger, Jon. "How Jeffery Boyd Took Priceline from Dot-Bomb to Highflier." *CNN Money,* September 11, 2012. tech.fortune.cnn.com/2012/09/11/priceline-jeffery-boyd/.

Bort, Julie. "Our Favorite Crazy Stunts from Salesforce Leader Marc Benioff." *Business Insider,* March 15, 2012. www.businessinsider.com/marc-benioff-salesforcecom-chief-has- pulled-some-crazy-stunts-2012-3?op=1#ixzz2eLsnA5K0.

Bryant, Adam. "Finding Purpose in Tunneling Through Granite." *New York Times,* April 13, 2013. www.nytimes.com/2013/04/14/business/guidewires-chief-on-embracing-adversity.html?pagewanted=all&_r=0.

Burke, Monte. "Five Guys Burgers: America's Fastest Growing Restaurant Chain." *Forbes,* July 18, 2012. www.forbes.com/sites/monteburke/2012/07/18/five-guys-burgers-americas-fastest-growing-restaurant-chain/.

Calloway, Joe. *Becoming a Category of One: How Extraordinary Companies Transcend Commodity and Defy Comparison.* Hoboken, NJ: John Wiley, 2009.

Christensen, Clayton. "Disruptive Innovation." www.claytonchristensen.com/key-concepts/#sthash.zukQNRiE.dpuf.

CRDF Global. GIST TechConnect Ideation online panel discussion, January 23, 2013. http://gist.crdfglobal.org/about-gist/events/2013/01/23/gist-techconnect-idea-creation-=-ideation.

Denning, Steve. "Clayton Christensen and the Innovators' Smackdown." *Forbes,* April 5, 2012. www.forbes.com/sites/stevedenning/2012/04/05/clayton-christensen-and-the-innovators-smackdown/.

Dennis, Felix. *How to Get Rich: The Distilled Wisdom of One of Britain's Wealthiest Self-Made Entrepreneurs.* London: Ebury Press, 2007.

Duggan, Daniel. "Manoj Bhargava on What Makes Successes Like 5-Hour Energy: Don't Waste Your Energy." *Crain's Detroit Business,* May 21, 2012. www.crainsdetroit.com/article/20120521/FREE/120529984/manoj-bhargava-on-what-makes-successes-like-5-hour-energy-don-t-waste-.

Duval, James. "Secrets of Success: How Cisco Outlasted Its Competitors." *CustomerTHINK Blog,* June 3, 2013. www.customerthink.com/blog/secrets_of_success_how_cisco_outlasted_its_competitors.

Eng, Dinah. "How We Got Started: Jim Koch: Samuel Adams's Beer Revolutionary." *CNN Money,* March 21, 2013. money.cnn.com/2013/03/21/smallbusiness/samual-adams-koch.pr.fortune/index.html.

Funding Universe. "Ask Jeeves, Inc. History." www.fundinguniverse.com/company-histories/ask-jeeves-inc-history/.

Funding Universe. "Priceline.com Incorporated History." www.funding universe.com/company-histories/priceline-com-incorporated-history/.

Giles, Lionel. *The Art of War by Sun Tzu: Special Edition.* El Paso, TX: El Paso Norte Press, 2005.

Gladwell, Malcolm. *The Tipping Point: How Little Things Can Make a Big Difference.* New York: Little, Brown, 2002.

Gobry, Pascal-Emmanuel. "10 Brilliant Startups That Failed Because They Were Ahead of Their Time." *Business Insider,* May 4, 2011. www.businessinsider.com/startup-failures-2011-5?op=1#ixzz2cJz7BT3I.

Goodman, Nadia. "James Dyson on Using Failure to Drive Success." *Entrepreneur,* November 5, 2012. www.entrepreneur.com/blog/224855#ixzz2e8H9o7ve.

Green, Sarah. "Who New CEOs Fire First." *HBR Blog Network,* July 8, 2013. blogs.hbr.org/hbr/hbreditors/2013/07/who_new_ceos_fire_first.html.

Gross, Daniel, "It's All Greek to Him: Chobani's Unlikely Success Story." *The Daily Beast,* June 12, 2013. www.thedailybeast.com/newsweek/2013/06/12/the-turkish-shepherd-behind-chobani.html.

Gruley, Bryan. "At Chobani, the Turkish King of Greek Yogurt." *Businessweek,* January 31, 2013. www.businessweek.com/articles/2013-01-31/at-chobani-the-turkish-king-of-greek-yogurt#p2.

Harbison, John R., Peter Pekar Jr., Albert Viscio, and David Maloney. *The Allianced Enterprise: Breakout Strategy for the New Millennium.* Los Angeles: Booz-Allen & Hamilton, 2000. www.smartalliancepartners.com/Images/Allianced%20Enterprise.pdf.

Hartung, Adam. "Netflix—The Turnaround Story of 2012!" *Forbes,* January 29, 2013. www.forbes.com/sites/adamhartung/2013/01/29/netflix-the-turnaround-story-of-2012/.

Heffernan, Margaret. "James Dyson on Creating a Vacuum That Actually, Well, Sucks." *Reader's Digest,* February 2009. www.rd.com/advice/work-career/james-dyson-on-creating-a-vacuum-that-actually-well-sucks/#ixzz2eKNGOMFq.

Heubeck, Elizabeth. "Wegmans' Grocery List for Success." *Baltimore Business Journal,* March 20, 2013. www.bizjournals.com/baltimore/print-edition/2012/05/25/wegmans-grocery-list-for-success.html?page= all.

Hsieh, Tony. *Delivering Happiness.* New York: Hachette Book Group, 2010.

Hsieh, Tony. "Your Culture Is Your Brand." *Zappos Blogs: CEO and COO Blog,* January 3, 2009. blogs.zappos.com/blogs/ceo-and-coo-blog/2009/ 01/03/your-culture-is-your-brand.

Huang, J. H. *Sun-Tzu: The Art of War—The New Translation.* New York: William Morrow, 1993.

Huynh, Thomas. *The Art of War—Spirituality for Conflict: Annotated and Explained.* Woodstock, VT: SkyLight Paths Publishing, 2012.

IBIS World. *Business Coaching in the U.S.: Market Research Report.* November 2013. www.ibisworld.com/industry/default.aspx?indid=1533.

"Interview Transcript: Meg Whitman, Ebay." *Financial Times,* June 18, 2006. www.ft.com/cms/s/2/f3ae81f8-fef8-11da-84f3-0000779e2340.html#axzz2dlJqgInb.

Keen, Andrew. "Keen On ... Clay Christensen: How to Escape the Innovator's Dilemma [TCTV]." *TechCrunch* video interview, April 2, 2012. techcrunch.com/2012/04/02/keen-on-clay-christensen-how-to-escape-the-innovators-dilemma-tctv/.

Krippendorff, Kaihan. "How Great Entrepreneurs Lure Their Competitors' Sheep Away." *Fast Company,* May 16, 2012. www.fastcompany.com/1837389/how-great-entrepreneurs-lure-their-competitors-sheep-away.

Leotin, Sylvie. "Atari: The Original Lean Startup." *VentureBeat,* October 13, 2010. venturebeat.com/2010/10/13/atari-the-original-lean-startup/.

MarketWatch Commentary. "Salesforce CEO Pulls Off Excellent Stunt." *MarketWatch,* October 5, 2011. www.marketwatch.com/story/salesforce-ceo-pulls-off-excellent-stunt-2011-10-05.

Maxwell, Scott, "Small Business Innovation Lessons from Salesforce.com." *OpenView Labs Blog,* January 31, 2013. labs.openviewpartners.com/small-business-innovation-lessons-from-salesforce-com/.

McMahan, Dana. "Craft Distillers Breaking into Kentucky's Billion-Dollar Bourbon Industry." *NBC News,* August 30, 2013. www.nbcnews.com/travel/craft-distillers-breaking-kentuckys-billion-dollar-bourbon-industry-8C11035874.

McNeilly, Mark R. *Sun Tzu and the Art of Modern Warfare.* New York: Oxford University Press, 2001.

Michaelson, Gerald A., and Steven Michaelson. *The Art of War for Managers: 5 Strategic Rules.* Avon, MA: Adams Media, 2010.

Nisen, Max, and Alexandra Mondalek. "Invaluable Advice from 18 of America's Top Small Business Owners." *Business Insider,* June 21, 2013. www.businessinsider.com/invaluable-advice-from-18-of-americas-top-small-business-owners-2013-6?op= 1#ixzz2cXyGkSmJ.

O'Connor, Clare. "The Mystery Monk Making Billions with 5-Hour Energy." *Forbes,* February 8, 2012. www.forbes.com/sites/clareoconnor/2012/02/08/manoj-bhargava-the-mystery-monk-making-billions-with-5-hour-energy/.

O'Hagan, Sean. "The Nine Lives of Felix Dennis." *The Guardian,* June 1, 2013. www.theguardian.com/media/2013/jun/02/nine-lives-of-felix-dennis.

Parr, Ben. "Here's Why Amazon Bought Zappos." *Mashable,* July 22, 2009. mashable. com/2009/07/22/amazon-bought-zappos/.

Pendleton, Devon. "Hidden Chobani Billionaire Emerges as Greek Yogurt Soars." *Bloomberg,* September 14, 2012. www.bloomberg.com/news/2012-09-14/hidden-chobani-billionaire-emerges-as-greek-yogurt-soars.html.

Penenberg, Adam L. "Reid Hoffman on PayPal's Pivoted Path to Success." *Fast Company,* including video interview of Hoffman, August 9, 2012. www.fastcompany. com/1837839/reid-hoffman-paypals-pivoted-path- success.

Pozin, Ilya, "9 Biggest Mistakes New Entrepreneurs Make." *Inc.,* July 20, 2013. www. inc.com/ilya-pozin/9-biggest-mistakes-you-will-make-as-a-new-entrepreneur.html.

Rohde, David. "The Anti-Walmart: The Secret Sauce of Wegmans Is People." *The Atlantic,* March 23, 2012. www.theatlantic.com/business/archive/2012/03/the-anti-walmart-the-secret-sauce-of-wegmans-is-people/ 254994/.

Salter, Chuck. "Failure Doesn't Suck." *Fast Company,* April 10, 2007. www.fastcompany. com/76673/failure-doesnt-suck-part-2.

Sambidge, Andy. "Yahoo!'s Maktoob Deal Valued at $175m—Report." *ArabianBusiness.com,* September 10, 2009. www.arabianbusiness.com/yahoo-s-maktoob-deal-valued-at-175m-report-12955.html#.UiSfYD_zjbw.

Sheetz-Runkle, Becky. *Sun Tzu for Women: The Art of War for Winning in Business.* Avon, MA: Adams Media, 2011.

Sonshi. "Interview with Marc Benioff." *Sonshi.com.* www.sonshi.com/benioff.html.

Taylor, Bill. "Why Zappos Pays New Employees to Quit—and You Should Too." *HBR Blog Network,* May 19, 2008. blogs.hbr.org/taylor/2008/05/why_zappos_pays_new_employees.html.

Thomas, Kathryn Quinn. "Golisano Built Paychex into a Success Story." *Rochester Business Journal,* October 8, 2004. www.rbj.net/article.asp?aID=149125.

Tice, Carol. "12 Ways to (Legally) Spy on Your Competitors." *Entrepreneur,* November 17, 2011. www.entrepreneur.com/article/220761#ixzz2cfCfx1pP.

Tobak, Steve. "David vs. Goliath: How Small Companies Make It Big." *Inc.,* March 27, 2013. www.inc.com/steve-tobak/david-vs-goliath-how-small-companies-make-itbig. html.

"Vacuum Makers Dyson, Hoover Settle Lawsuit." *Appliance Magazine.* October 10, 2002. www.appliancemagazine.com/news.php?article= 3691.

Vitello, Paul. "Elmer T. Lee, Whose Premium Bourbon Revived an Industry, Dies at 93." *New York Times,* July 21, 2013. www.nytimes.com/2013/ 07/22/business/elmer-t-lee-whose-premium-bourbon-revived-an-industry- dies-at-93.html?_r=0.

Wegmans corporate website. "Frequently Asked Questions." www.wegmans.com. www.wegmans.com/webapp/wcs/stores/servlet/FAQDetailView?storeId=10052&catalog Id=10002&langId=-1&faqCategory=AboutWegmans# question_12.

Welch, Liz. "How I Did It: Jerry Murrell, Five Guys Burgers and Fries." *Inc.,* April 1, 2010. www.inc.com/magazine/20100401/jerry-murrell-five-guys-burgers-and-fries.html.

Zappos Insights. www.zapposinsights.com/ www.zappos.com.

INDEX